Easy Steps to Speed Up Windows® XP:
Now That You've Had Windows® XP for Awhile, How to Make It Run Faster

ISBN: 1-4196-2842-9
ISBN-13: 978-1419628429

Visit www.booksurge.com to order additional copies.

Easy Steps to Speed Up Windows® XP: Now That You've Had Windows® XP for Awhile, How to Make It Run Faster

Michael Palmer

2007

Easy Steps to Speed Up Windows® XP:
Now That You've Had Windows® XP for Awhile, How to Make It Run Faster

Table of Contents

What This Book Can Do for You

Remember when you first purchased your Windows XP computer and every mouse click produced a quick result? Remember when each time you turned on your computer it started right up without taking forever—and when you opened a program it was ready to go without delay? You bought your computer to do things faster and better, but now you spend more and more time waiting on the computer. The growing number of minutes you spend waiting may even add stress, particularly if you are already behind or in a hurry.

If you have Windows XP and find you are spending more time waiting on your computer, this book can help. It can also help you if there are particular computer tasks that have never met your expectations for quick response, such as opening a folder or using the Internet.

No matter what level of computer user you are, this book gives you easy steps to speed up your computer. And because you are busy with many things in your life, the book is written in a brief and direct step-by-step format, similar to a cookbook. You don't have to be a computer expert to use this book. You only have to have an interest in making your computer run faster.

I dedicate this book in memory of Edward and Helen Palmer

Chapter 1

Jump Start Your Computer: Easy Steps to a Faster Startup

If you're frustrated by a computer that is slow to start, you're not alone. When it was new, your computer started right up—no need to go make a cup of coffee while waiting for your computer to start. After several months you've added more software, more Internet features, and worked on more files. Your computer seems to take longer and longer to start up—as you impatiently sit in front of it listening to the hard drive work and watching the little hourglass.

You don't have to be an expert or even very experienced with Windows XP to revitalize your computer's startup. You only have to be interested in having a computer that is faster to start and be willing to follow the easy steps provided in this chapter.

Reducing Start-Up Program Clutter

One reason why you have to wait while your computer boots is that the computer is starting more programs in the background than it did when you first got it. Each time you install new software, the installation process may set up your computer to start programs when the computer boots. You might see these programs as new icons in your taskbar. Or, the programs may run in the background without your knowledge. There is no reason for many of these programs to automatically load at startup. You can start them when you want them from the Start menu. As you put more software on your computer, a lot of unnecessary clutter builds up in your startup programs that can cost you time that could be used enjoying the real benefits of your computer. Fortunately, there are steps you can take to get rid of the startup program clutter. Use the tips in the following sections to remove the clutter from your startup.

Unclutter Your Startup Folder

Programs in your Startup Folder start when you start your computer and log in. The more programs that are in this folder, the longer it takes for your computer to start up. You may find there are several programs you don't need to have in your Startup Folder, because you can always start them later.

To remove programs in the Startup Folder:

Tip: For all of the steps mentioned in this book, it is best to close any open windows or active programs before you start.

1. Click the **Start** button.
2. Click **My Computer**.
3. Double-click **Local Disk (C:)** as in Figure 1-1.

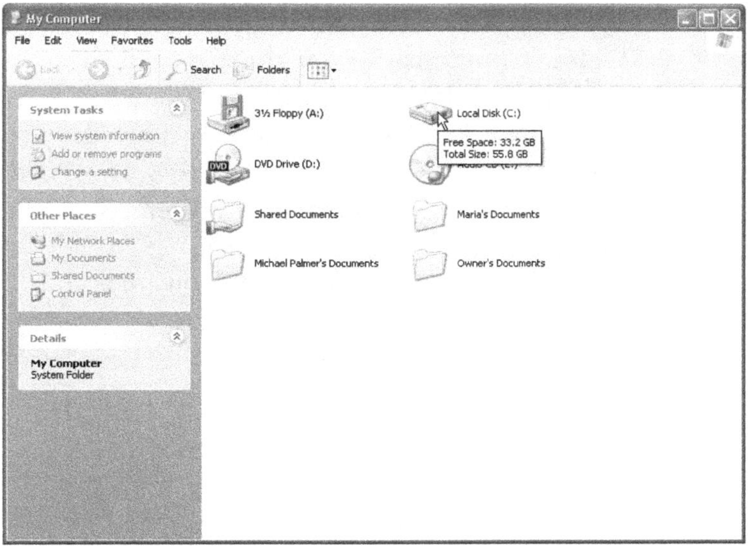

Figure 1-1: Selecting Local Disk (C:)

4. Double-click **Documents and Settings**.
5. Double-click the folder with the name of your user account.
6. Double-click the **Start Menu** folder.
7. Double-click the **Programs** folder.
8. Double-click the **Startup** folder.
9. Select any shortcuts you want to delete. Don't worry—you're not deleting the actual programs, only shortcuts to the programs. You know it is a shortcut because there is a semicircular up arrow in a white box on the icon. One way to delete a shortcut is to right-click the shortcut and then click **Delete** on the menu (see Figure 1-2 and don't worry if your menu has some different options than in the figure, you'll still have a Delete option).

If you see a Confirm Shortcut Delete box, click **Delete Shortcut**. Repeat this for each shortcut you want to delete. Another way is to press and hold the **Ctrl** key and while holding down the Ctrl key click each shortcut you want to delete. After you select all of the shortcuts to delete, press the **Del** key to delete them all at once.

10. Close the Startup window when you are done.

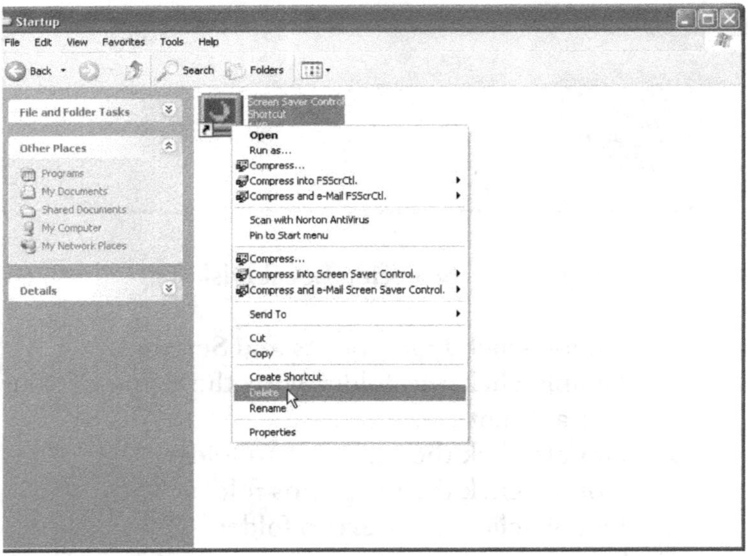

Figure 1-2: Deleting a shortcut in the Startup folder

Unclutter Additional Startup Programs

Besides the program shortcuts in the Startup folder, there are other programs started through your computer's startup configuration. You can increase the startup speed of your computer by removing some of these other programs that are automatically started when you start your computer.

In addition to programs, there are many services that start when you boot your computer. You might think of services as programs that enable other programs to run on your computer. For example, when you use the print program to print a file, the printer program uses the print spooler service. In another example, each time you connect new hardware to your computer, the Add Hardware program uses the Plug and Play service to automatically detect the new hardware.

Some services are absolutely needed to run your computer, such as the Server and Workstation services. There are other services you may never use. For example, if you never burn CDs, then you don't use the IMAPI CD-Burning COM Service. When you choose not to automatically start unused services, you enjoy two advantages: (1) your computer starts faster and (2) your computer is safer from intruders. Network and Internet intruders can use started services as a backdoor into your computer. When you shut down services you don't need, you shut down intruders' access.

Windows XP (as well as earlier versions of Windows) offers the Microsoft System Configuration utility, *msconfig*, to disable specific programs and services from starting automatically when you start your computer. When you disable unused programs and services, you can give your computer a significant speed boost.

To use *msconfig* for disabling programs and services:

1. Click the **Start** button.
2. Click **Run.**
3. Enter **msconfig** in the Open box and click **OK** (see Figure 1-3).

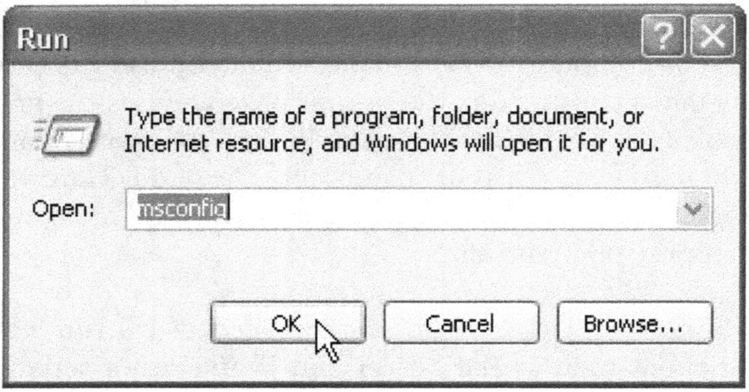

Figure 1-3: Running the *msconfig* program

4. Click the **Startup** tab.
5. Listed under the Startup Item column are programs your computer automatically starts when it boots (see Figure 1-4)—a lot of programs with odd names like ctfmon that you probably haven't got a clue about. The check in the box in front of a program means that program is selected to start automatically. If you remove the check from in front of a program, it will not load at startup. Removing the check only means that the program will not start when you start the computer. You can still start the program later, such as by clicking its icon on your desktop.

There are several programs you should not uncheck, because they are used by your system. Table 1-1 lists examples of programs you should leave checked (your computer may not have all of these programs, depending on the software you've installed). One rule of thumb is to leave checked programs that are shown to be in the Windows\System32 file when you look under the Command column. Also, if you are unsure of what a program does, it is safer to leave it checked.

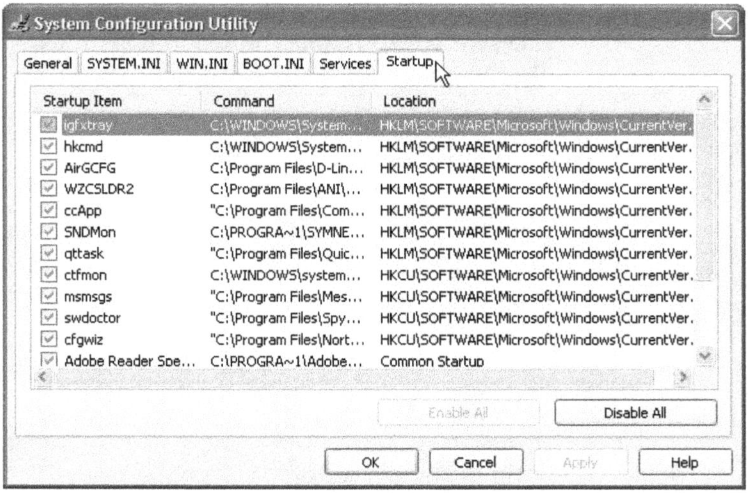

Figure 1-4: The *msconfig* Startup tab

Program	Explanation
airCCFG	Used for wireless communications (you can disable if you don't use wireless)
ccApp	Used by some security software
ctfmon	Used by Microsoft Office programs and runs in the background
hkcmd	Hot Key Command Module used by Intel hardware in your computer for graphics reproduction on your screen
igfxtray	Intel graphics tray used by Intel hardware in your computer for graphics reproduction on your screen
WZCSLDR2	Used for wireless communications (you can disable if you don't use wireless)

Table 1-1: Startup Programs Your System Needs

6. Click the **Services** tab. The services that your computer starts during the startup process are listed under the Service column (see Figure 1-5).

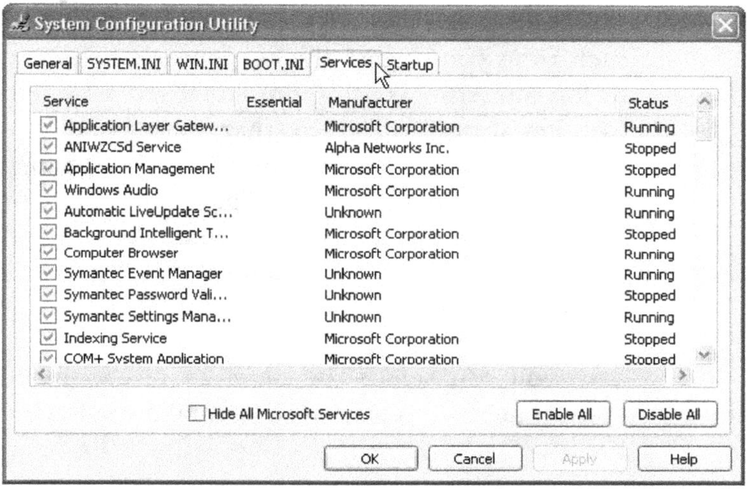

Figure 1-5: The *msconfig* Services tab

7. You can disable one or more services from starting when your computer starts. To do this, remove the check in the box for a specific service. When you are finished removing checks, click **OK**. Ensure that any open programs or files are closed and then click **Yes** to reboot your computer. Example services to consider disabling include those listed after this step. *Be careful when you disable services, so you do not disable one that you need, however note that Windows XP won't let you disable a service it requires.* One way to proceed is to delete one or two services, click **OK**, and click **Restart** to restart your computer to make sure it works properly. Then repeat deleting one or two more services, click **OK**, and click **Restart** to restart. Continue until you've finished disabling

the services you want to have disabled. Note that each time you restart the computer you'll need to log on. After you log on, you'll see a System Configuration Utility box that warns you have used the System Configuration Utility to change how the computer starts. Check the box for **Don't show this message or launch the System Configuration Utility when Windows starts.** Click **OK**. After you click **OK**, you automatically go into the System Configuration Utility. From here you can select the Services tab to make more changes, or close the System Configuration Utility.

Services to consider disabling include:

- *Audio Device:* Consider disabling if you have no audio devices, such as speakers, connected to your computer.
- *Automatic Live Update Scheduler:* Consider disabling if you prefer to manually initiate updating software, such as obtaining new definitions for virus scanning software. One advantage of doing updates manually is that you can choose when to update, so that the computer is not busy with other tasks at the time of the updates.
- *Computer Browser:* Consider disabling if you do not have network or Internet access.
- *DHCP Client:* Consider disabling *only* if you don't have network or Internet access.
- *DNS Client:* Consider disabling *only* if you do not have network or Internet access.
- *Fast User Switching Compatibility:* Consider disabling if you don't have multiple accounts on

your computer so that you can share its use with others (see Chapter 5 for more information about fast user switching).

- *Help and Support:* Consider disabling if you do not plan to consult the help documentation available for Windows XP.
- *IMAPI CD-Burning COM Service:* Consider disabling if you do not burn CDs.
- *LiveUpdate:* Consider disabling if you prefer to manually update software.
- *NetMeeting Remote Desktop Sharing:* Consider disabling if you are not planning to use remote desktop sharing (disabling is a good security practice).
- *Network Location Awareness (NLA):* Consider disabling if you are not connected to a network.
- *Network Provisioning Service:* Consider disabling if you are not connected to a network or do not use XML (XML is commonly used by Internet Web sites).
- *Portable Media Serial Number Service:* Consider disabling if you do not have a portable media player.
- *Print Spooler:* Consider disabling if there is no printer connected to your computer.
- *Remote Access Auto Connection Manger:* Consider disabling if you are not connected to a network.
- *Remote Access Connection Manager:* Consider disabling if you are not connected to a network.
- *Remote Desktop Help Session Manager:* Consider disabling if you do not anticipate enabling Remote Assistance in Windows XP. (Remote Assistance enables a computer support person to remotely

access your computer via a network as a way to help you solve a computer problem.)

- *Smart Card:* Consider disabling if you do not use a smart card to access your computer (a smart card looks similar to a credit card).
- *Terminal Services:* Consider disabling if others don't access your computer remotely and if you don't use Remote Assistance (see also Remote Access Connection Manager).
- *Uninterruptible Power Supply:* Consider disabling if you do not have an uninterruptible power supply (UPS) connected to your computer so the computer can manage its use (a UPS keeps your computer running through a power failure or brownout).
- *WebClient:* Consider disabling if you do not have Internet or network access.
- *Windows Audio:* Consider disabling if you do not use audio functions on your computer, such as for playing music.
- *Windows Image Acquisition:* Consider disabling if you have no scanners or cameras attached to your computer.

Tip: If you want to learn more about services, use the Computer Management tool. Click Start, right-click My Computer, and click Manage. In the Computer Management window, double-click Services and Applications in the left pane and then click Services in the left pane. Click a service and read its description.

If you disable a service and you discover you need it after all, you can always go back into the System Configuration Utility to enable it. If you have problems when you restart the computer, you can go back to using all of the services you disabled. In the System Configuration Utility (*msconfig*), open the General tab and you'll notice that Selective Startup is selected. Click "Normal Startup—load all device drivers and services" (but don't select this if your computer is running without problems).

Removing Your Desktop Background

Another action you can take to reduce the startup time is to remove your desktop background. That background photo of your favorite nature scene or family or friends is often a large graphics file that takes memory that could be used to speed up other activities, such as starting up and running programs. If you discover you are not looking at the desktop very often because you're normally in a word processor or another application, consider removing the background.

To remove the background, use the following steps:

1. Right-click the background on your desktop (but not on an open window or icon).
2. Click **Properties** in the menu.
3. Click the **Desktop** tab.
4. If necessary, scroll to the top of the list and click **None** in the Background: box (see Figure 1-6).
5. Click **OK**.

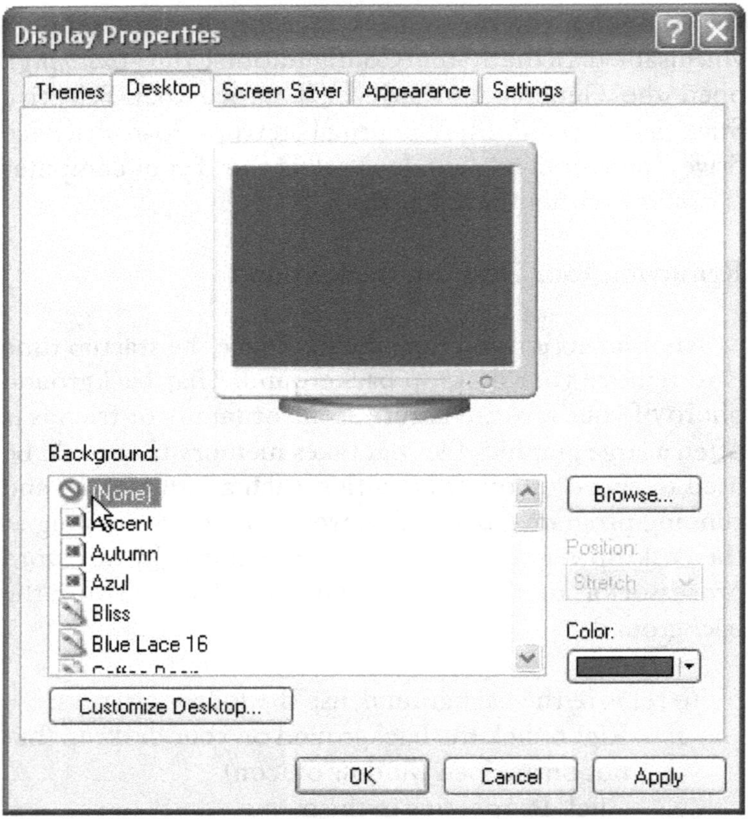

Figure 1-6: Configuring to use no background

Simplifying Visual Effects

Your computer may have one or more visual effects configured. These can include fade effects, shadows, animation and other effects. The computer's startup time and performance after startup can be slowed down by using these visual effects. One way to increase your computer's speed is to remove some or all of the visual effects.

Use the following steps to configure the visual effects on your computer:

1. Click **Start**.
2. Click **Control Panel**.
3. In the left pane of Control Panel, if you see *Switch to Classic View* then you are in the Category View of the Control Panel tool—stay in this view and click the **Performance and Maintenance** category, then click the **System** icon. If instead you see *Switch to Category View* in the left pane of Control Panel—stay in this view and double-click the **System** icon.
4. Click the **Advanced** tab.
5. In the area labeled Performance, click the **Settings** button.
6. Ensure the **Visual Effects** tab is displayed, and if not, click it.
7. If you want to adjust for the best performance, click the option button for **Adjust for best performance**. Keep in mind that if you select this option, your display effects will be much plainer. An alternative approach, as shown in Figure 1-7 is to click **Custom** and then to select the specific visual effects you want to use (you'll have to click boxes to remove checks, which removes the visual effects associated with those unchecked boxes). Some examples of visual effects you might leave are: Show shadows under menus, Show shadows under mouse pointer, and Use visual styles on windows and buttons.
8. Click **OK** in the Performance Options box.
9. Click **OK** in the System Properties box.
10. Close the Performance and Maintenance or Control Panel window.

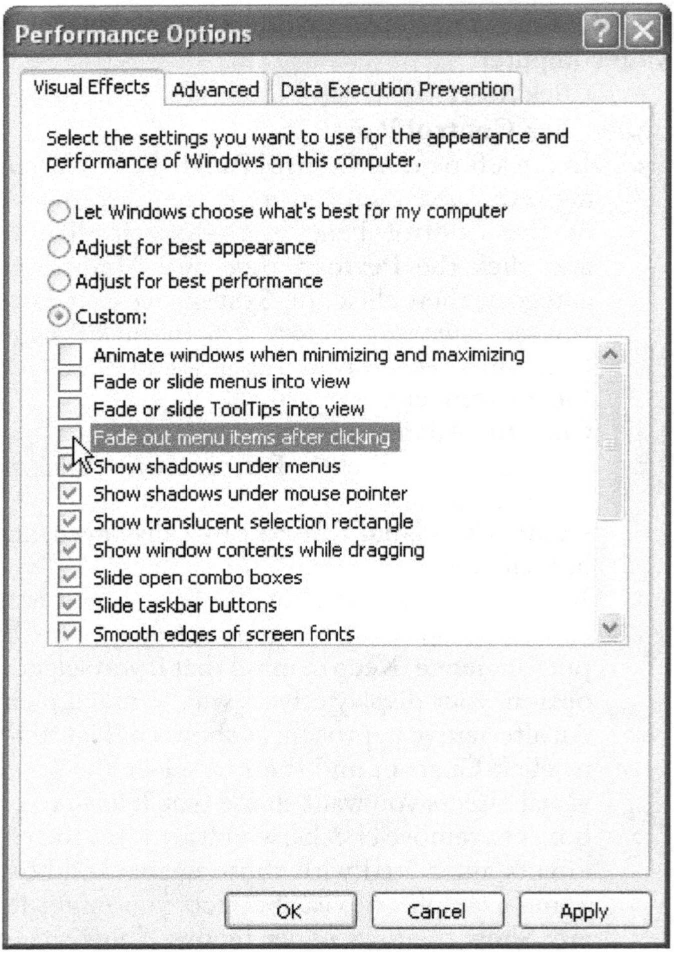

Figure 1-7: Customizing visual effects

Scanning for Viruses and Spyware

There are many forms of malicious software (malware) that can threaten the integrity of computer files and slow down a computer. Some common forms of malware are viruses, worms, Trojan horses, and spyware. A virus is a program that can replicate through many places on your computer, such as in files and disks. In the process, a virus not only can damage files, but may also bring your computer's startup process and speed to its knees.

A worm is a program that keeps creating more and more new files. It may create files so quickly that your computer will barely start up or work. A Trojan horse is a program that is disguised to look useful. You might download a Trojan horse from the Internet because it appears to perform interesting functions, such as displaying an animated cartoon or providing a free word processor. In reality the Trojan horse performs harm. For example, the Trojan horse may give an attacker backdoor access to your computer.

Spyware is software that enables someone to collect information about how you use your computer. It may be used by an attacker to monitor your Internet purchases in an attempt to obtain your credit card number. Another use of spyware is by advertisers to gain information about your interests when you are using the Internet. Besides invading your privacy, spyware programs can slow down the startup and operation of your computer.

Plan to purchase and regularly use software that scans your computer for viruses, worms, Trojan horses, and spyware. The following are examples of companies that sell scanning software:

- Lavasoft offers Ad-Aware and Lavasoft Personal

Firewall. Visit their Web site at *www.lavasoft.com*.
- McAfee sells Anti-Virus, Anti-Hacker & Anti-Spyware, and Internet Security Suite. Go to *www.mcafee.com* to find out more about these products.
- PC Tools Software offers products such as Spyware Doctor and PC Tools Antivirus. Visit their Web site at *www.pctools.com*.
- Safer-Networking.org provides Spybot Search & Destroy. Find out more at *www.safer-networking.org*.
- Symantec provides Norton Antivirus, Norton Internet Security, and Norton Personal Firewall. Symantec's Web site is *www.symantec.com*.

Some of these vendors offer versions of their software that you can download for a trial period, so you can decide how you like the software before you purchase it. Also, you can download free versions of Ad-Aware and Spybot Search & Destroy for individual computer use.

None of these programs offer 100% protection. But you can come close to this goal by using two programs on your computer. For example, you might purchase an antivirus scanner from PCTools, Symantec, or McAfee plus use the free version of Ad-Aware or Spybot Search & Destroy. Another way to approach 100% protection is to frequently update your antivirus/spyware software. All of the vendors mentioned here provide an update service so that you obtain the latest updates to combat new malware.

Checking Your Disk Files for Errors

Sometimes an operating system or another file can become corrupted, such as after a power failure unexpectedly shuts down your computer. Also, important indexes used by your file system may be damaged or there may be a bad sector on a disk. These situations can cause some or all of the following problems:

- Slow system startup
- A fatal error screen ("blue screen of death") after you start your computer
- Slow response after you start your computer

In many cases, you don't need a computer expert to fix a corrupted system file, an index, or a damaged disk sector. You can use the same basic tool an expert would use, the Checkdisk utility or *chkdsk*.

Start by running *chkdsk* to see if your disk files have any errors. *chkdsk* can find errors while you are logged on, but it won't fix the errors because your computer and disks are always busy running programs in the background. If you see that *chkdsk* has found an error, you can instruct *chkdsk* to run again the next time you start the computer, so it can lock your disk and fix the errors before you log on. Here is how to run *chkdsk*:

1. Close all windows and active programs.
2. Click **Start**, point to **All Programs**, point to **Accessories**, and click **Command Prompt**.
3. You see the Command Prompt Window. Your cursor should be blinking after a command prompt line, such as C:\Documents and Settings\ *your accountname*>. Type in the command **chkdsk** and press **Enter**.

4. Give your system some time to complete the *chkdsk* process.
5. Examine the chkdsk report on the screen to determine if any errors are reported (see Figure 1-8). If there are no errors reported, close the Command Prompt window.

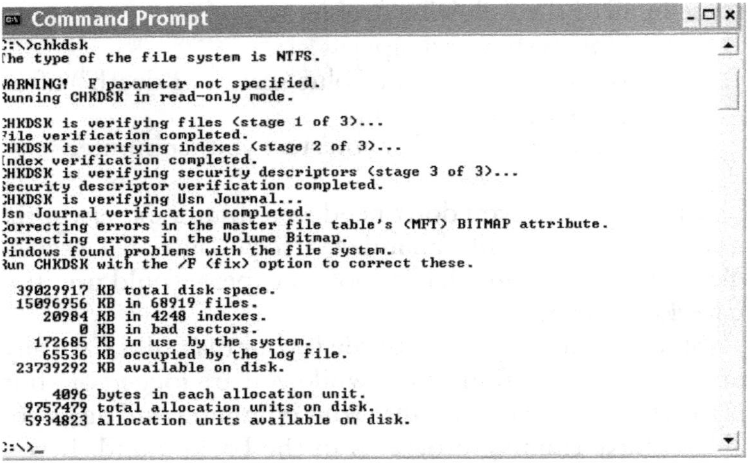

Figure 1-8: Viewing the *chkdsk* report

6. If there are one or more errors (damaged files, indexes, or sectors), type in **chkdsk /f** and press **Enter**. The /f is a "switch" used with *chkdsk* that instructs the utility to lock the disk and fix any errors that it finds.
7. Type **y** and press **Enter** so that *chkdsk* will run and fix your errors the next time the computer starts up.
8. Close the Command Prompt window.
9. Restart your computer. Click **Start**, click **Turn**

Off Computer, and click **Restart**. (If you are using Windows XP without certain updates your restart procedure may be to click **Start**, click **Shut Down**, select **Restart**, and click **OK**.)

10. When your computer restarts you'll see a screen that shows *chkdsk* is running.

Cleaning Out the My Recent Documents, Temp, and History Folders

Each time your computer starts up it examines the contents of the My Recent Documents, Temp, and History folders for your account. For a faster start up, consider periodically deleting the contents of these folders. The My Recent Documents folder is used to track documents you have recently opened. If you don't use this option from the Start menu, consider periodically deleting the list of recently opened documents. The Temp folder is used to store temporary files used by programs and update processes and which are often not automatically deleted. The History folder contains a history used by Internet Explorer of folders and Web sites that you have accessed on your computer.

To delete the contents of the My Recent Documents, Temp, and History folders:

1. Ensure that all programs, files, and folders are closed.
2. Click **Start** and click **My Computer**.
3. Double-click **Local Disk (C:)**.
4. Double-click the **Documents and Settings** folder.
5. Double-click the folder with your account name.
6. Double-click the **My Recent Documents** folder.

Notice that it is likely filled with shortcuts to files and folders you have recently accessed.

7. Press **Ctrl-A** to select all entries in the My Recent Documents folder.
8. Press **Del**.
9. Click **Yes** to confirm you want to delete the files. If you see a Confirm File Delete box that asks if you really want to delete a system file, such as Desktop.ini, click **No**.
10. Click the **Back** arrow to leave the My Recent Documents folder and go back to the folder with your account name.
11. Double-click the **Local Settings** folder.
12. Double-click the **History** folder.
13. Press **Ctrl-A** to select all entries in the History folder.
14. Press **Del**.
15. Click **Yes** to confirm you want to delete the files.
16. Click the **Back** arrow to leave the History folder and go back to the Local Settings folder.
17. Double-click the **Temp** folder.
18. Press **Ctrl-A** to select all entries in the Temp folder.
19. Press **Del**.
20. Click **Yes** to confirm you want to delete the files. (After you click Yes, you may see an error message that a particular file could not be deleted. If you see this message, right-click an open area on the taskbar, click **Task Manager**, and on the **Applications** tab close all applications other than Temp. To close an application click it and then click **End Task**. Repeat Steps 18—21. Also,

if you see a message that a particular file is a read-only file click **Yes** to delete it.)

21. Close the Temp folder's window.

Another way to clean out the contents of the My Recent Documents folder is in the properties of the Start menu. Also, if you want to disable the folder you can do this in the same place:

1. Right-click the **Start** menu and click **Properties**.
2. Click the **Start Menu** tab, if it is not already selected.
3. Click the **Customize** button.
4. Click the **Advanced** tab.
5. Click the **Clear List** button to clean out the My Recent Documents folder. Do this this even if you plan to disable My Recent Documents, so the My Recent Documents folder is empty (you can also later delete the My Recent Documents folder if you plan to disable this function in Step 6).
6. If you want to disable My Recent Documents, click to remove the check in the box for **List my most recently opened documents** (see Figure 1-9).

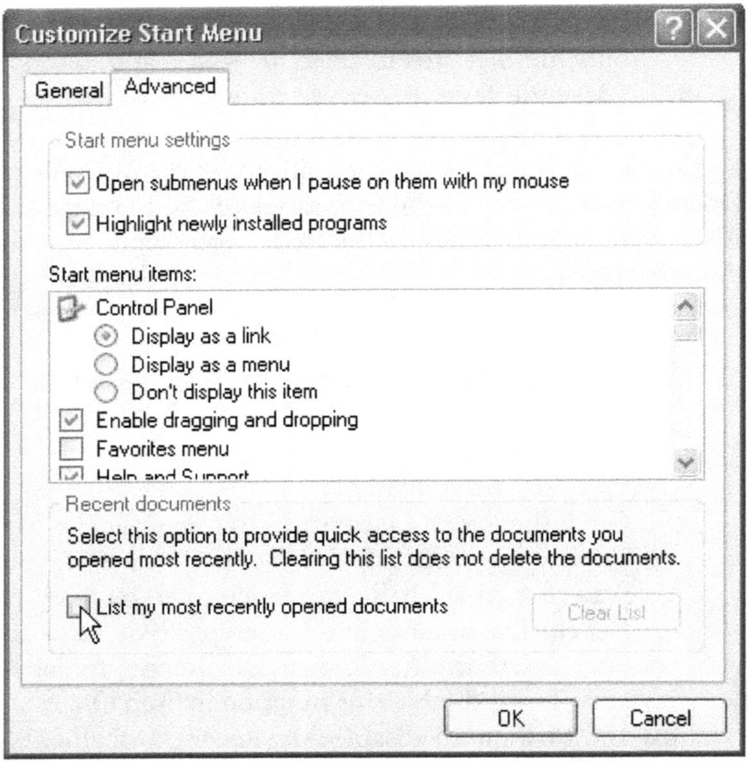

Figure 1-9: Disabling My Recent Documents

7. Click **OK** to close the Customize Start Menu dialog box.
8. Click **OK** to close the Taskbar and Start Menu Properties dialog box.

Disabling Devices You Don't Use

Your computer may have hardware settings configured for devices that you don't use such as gaming devices, specialized video devices (including viewing TV through your computer), wireless (Firewire) connections for a keyboard or mouse, MIDI devices for creating music, and so on. There is software associated with each device that your computer may load at startup. Also, there may be a port or device card in your computer that it must initiate when the computer starts.

Disabling or even removing devices you don't use will help your computer start and run faster. Windows XP offers the Device Manager tool for enabling and disabling devices. Device Manager is also used to remove the software to run devices. Try the following steps to disable or remove an unused device:

1. Click **Start**.
2. Right-click **My Computer** and click **Manage**.
3. Click **Device Manager** under System Tools.
4. Double-click any device types that may contain devices you can remove. For example, you might double-click *Sound, video and game controllers*. Under this device type, look for devices you are certain that are not used, such as a device listed as a game controller. (Another possibility is if your computer has network adapters for wired and wireless networks. You might use one or the other but not both, such as only wireless networking. Still another option might be to look under ports and disable a modem card you do not use.) After you select the device category and have displayed the devices under it, right-click the device you want to disable and click **Disable** (see Figure 1-10). If you see the message "Disabling this device will cause it to stop functioning. Do you really want

to disable it?"—click **Yes**. Note that some devices that your computer needs do not have the disable option and so this prevents you from disabling a device you need. Also notice that there may be an option to *Uninstall*. Before you uninstall a device, first disable it and run your computer for several days to make sure you don't need the device. Once you are certain you don't need it, go back and uninstall the device.

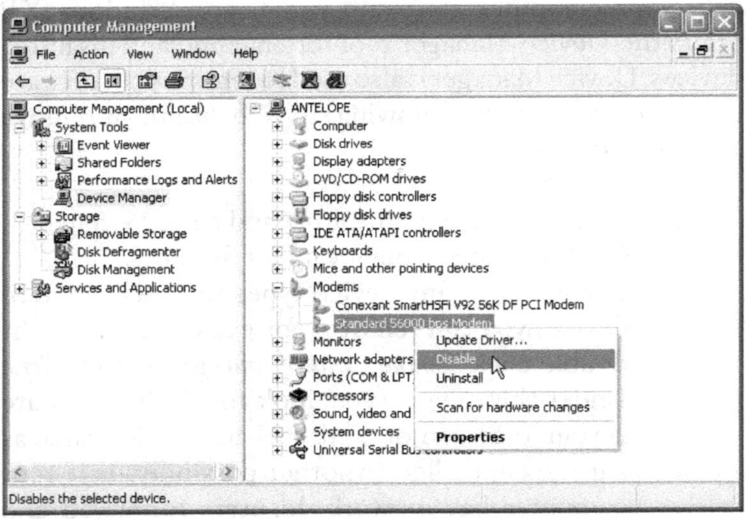

Figure 1-10: Disabling a dial-up modem in Device Manager

5. Once you select to disable a device, click **Yes**.
6. After you click Yes, you'll notice that the device is now displayed with a red **X** through it. (You can re-enable the device by right-clicking it and clicking Enable.)
7. Close the Computer Management screen.

Tips for Those Who Want to Work with the Registry

You can "tune" the Registry in Windows operating systems to help speed the response of your computer, including the startup time. The Registry is a database that houses all kinds of information about your operating system and computer including:

- Configuration
- Startup tasks
- Devices connected to the computer
- Software setup
- Operating system information

Windows XP (and other versions of Windows) comes with an editor called *regedit* that you can use to access and change information in the Registry. If you can run and use programs in Windows XP, you can quickly learn to use *regedit*.

Tip: You'll hear all kinds of warnings about working with the Registry, because it is possible to make changes in Registry areas that can keep your system from working properly or that even prevent your computer from booting. However, making some changes to the Registry yourself can yield good benefits, such as enabling your computer to boot and work faster. Also, Registry changes are easy to make. The important factor to remember is to avoid making changes on your own with no prior instructions to guide your way.

Automatically Defragment System Files

Your system will start faster when critical system files are located near the beginning of your hard drive and when they are next to one another, or contiguous. Your computer starts out this way, but over time as files are created, modified, and deleted, they are moved around and the system files may be separated in location on the disk. By default, most installations of Windows XP automatically run a specialized process that rearranges or defragments the system files so they are stored side by side in one place near the beginning of the disk. This makes them faster to access. However, sometimes the system file defragmentation process is disabled from starting automatically, such as by a power failure or virus. If your startup is slow, you can edit the Registry to make sure this process is set to run automatically each time your computer starts.

To configure your system to automatically defragment the system files at startup:

1. Click **Start**.
2. Click **Run**.
3. Enter **regedit** and click **OK**.
4. Double-click the **HKEY_LOCAL_MACHINE** folder in the left pane.
5. Double-click the **SOFTWARE** folder in the left pane (see Figure 1-11).

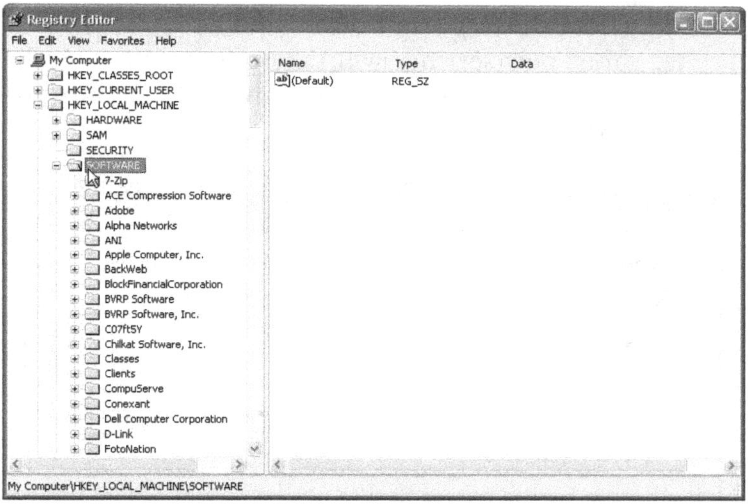

Figure 1-11: Selecting the SOFTWARE folder in regedit

6. Double-click the **Microsoft** folder in the left pane.
7. Double-click the **Dfrg** folder in the left pane.
8. Double-click the **BootOptimizeFunction** folder in the left pane.
9. In the right pane under the Name column, find Enable. The value in the Data column for Enable should be Y, which enables the automatic system file defragmentation process. If the value is Y, you can close the Registry Editor window.
10. If the value is not Y, you want to modify this setting. Double-click **Enable** and enter **Y** for the **Value data:** entry. Click **OK** (see Figure 1-12).

Tip: If you want to continue with the Enable Your Computer to Shut Down Faster steps, proceed to Step 4 in that section.

11. Close the Registry Editor window.
12. Your new settings will take effect following the next time you shut down and then restart the computer.

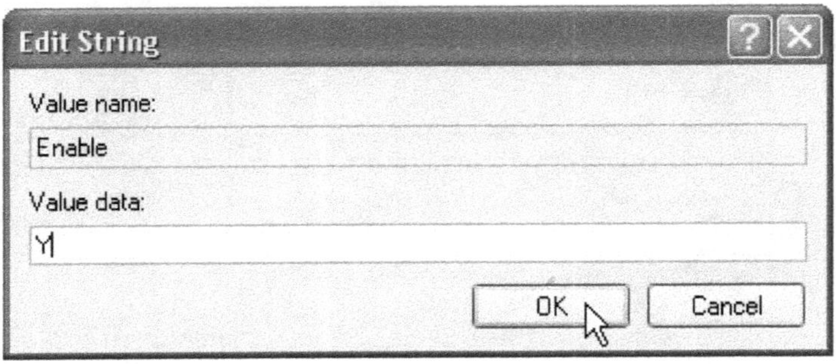

Figure 1-12: Configuring the Enable setting

Enable Your Computer to Shut Down Faster

Have you wondered why your computer takes so long to shut down? A common reason is that your computer is waiting to shut down programs and processes that are still running. Even when you close windows and other programs before you shut down, there are still open programs running in the background. When you shut down, Windows sends instructions to close open programs and program processes. If a program or process does not close right away, Windows waits a specified amount of time before it forces the program to close by "killing" its process(es).

There are several places in the Registry in which you can reduce the time Windows waits to kill programs and processes. Try the following Registry changes to improve the shutdown time of your computer:

1. Click **Start**.
2. Click **Run**.
3. Enter **regedit** and click **OK**.
4. Double-click the **HKEY_LOCAL_MACHINE** folder in the left pane.
5. Double-click the **SYSTEM** folder in the left pane.
6. Double-click the **CurrentControlSet** folder in the left pane.
7. Double-click the **Control** folder in the left pane.
8. Double-click **WaitToKillServiceTimeout** in the right pane.
9. The **Value data:** box typically has a high delay value, such as 20000. Remove this value and enter 200, which significantly reduces the delay time. Click **OK**.
10. Double-click the **HKEY_CURRENT_USER** folder in the left pane.
11. Double-click the **Control Panel** folder in the left pane.
12. Double-click the **Desktop** folder in the left pane.
13. Double-click **HungAppTimeout** in the right pane and change this value to 200 (the default is likely to be 5000). Click **OK**.
14. Double-click **WaitToKillAppTimeout** in the right pane and change the value to 200 (20000 is generally the default). Click **OK**.
15. Close the Registry Editor window.
16. Your new settings will take effect following the

next time you shut down and then restart the computer.

Chapter 2

Help Your Programs Run Faster

After your computer is started, you want to open up programs and use them as soon as possible. You don't want to wait for menus that are slow to display or programs that take forever to start. And when you are using an application you want a snappy response. After all, aren't computers supposed to make you more productive so you can finish your work and have more time for trouble-free computer recreation?

There are all kinds of steps you can take to help your programs run more quickly and efficiently, which should make your whole computer run faster. Some of these steps involve cleaning out files you don't need. Other steps involve making simple tweaks to help your computer and its programs run faster.

Cleaning Out Files You Don't Need

It does not take much time for your computer to accumulate a heavy load of files you don't use and don't need, especially temporary files, which can occupy disk space and bog down the computer. This is like a hiker carrying a 50-pound pack, of which only 10 pounds is actually used for hiking. The hiker can go faster and farther if he gets rid of unnecessary items and trims down the weight.

Programs that you run on a daily basis often leave temporary files on your computer. This is especially true if you use Microsoft Office software, including Word, Excel, Access, PowerPoint, and Publisher. Other programs, such as Web browsers, drawing software, publishing software, design software, and others leave temporary files. Temporary files are also left on your computer when you install software.

There are two reasons for regularly removing temporary files:

1. Temporary files can slow down your computer and applications.
2. Temporary files take up valuable disk space.

Temporary files can interfere with the smooth operation of your computer programs in several ways. For example, temporary files created by Microsoft Word may slow down Word when it starts. Word examines these files to determine if an earlier Word session was interrupted, in case it needs to reconstruct and display a particular file. Sometimes a temporary file created previously in Word will conflict with one you are currently working on. As you are working in Word, your session may slow or halt and you may get an error message that says your currently opened file is damaged or corrupted. A common solution is to close Word and delete temporary files.

Web browsers leave many temporary files on your computer. Some e-mail systems also use temporary files to store attachments. If you take steps to clean up these files, the applications that created them will work better.

Another reason for clearing out temporary files is the practical matter of disk space. A nearly full disk does not work at peak performance because the mechanisms used to search for and find files must work harder and take more time.

The sections that follow give you tips for finding and deleting unnecessary files.

Perform a Quick File Cleanup

Many temporary files either start with the tilde (~) character or end with the .tmp extension. You can perform a quick cleanup by searching for all files that match this description and then deleting them. Try the following steps for a quick cleanup:

Tip: It's best to close any open windows or active programs before you start the steps presented in this chapter.

1. Click the **Start** button.
2. Click **My Computer**.
3. Double-click **Local Disk (C:)** or another drive that you want to clean.
4. Click the **Search** button near the top of the window.
5. In the left pane, click **All files and folders** (see Figure 2-1).

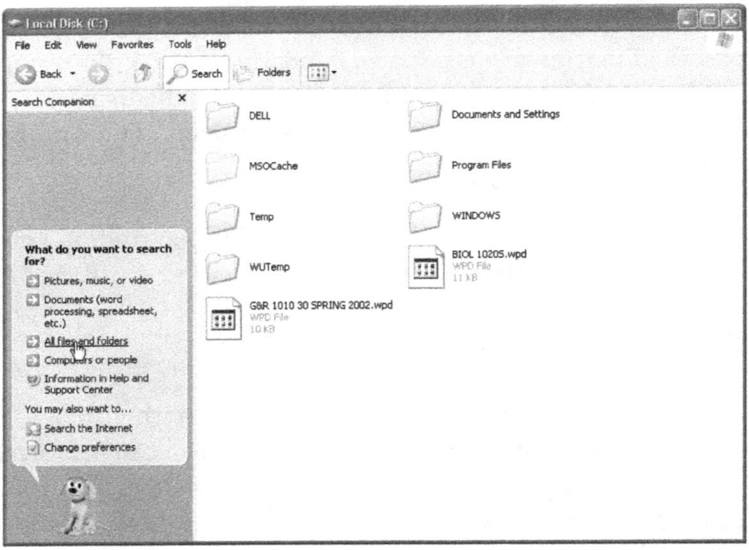

Figure 2-1: Searching for temporary files

6. In the **All or part of the file name:** box, enter ~* to search for all files starting with a tilde. The * acts like a wildcard in this instance so that it searches for files with any characters after the ~ at the beginning of the file name.
7. Click the **Search** button in the bottom of the left pane.
8. When the search is done examine the list. If all items found start with ~, press **Ctrl+A** to select all of the items found in the search. If all items don't start with ~, press and hold the **Ctrl** key and click each of the items that starts with ~ (so that each is highlighted). Press the **Del** key and click **Yes** to confirm you want to delete these temporary files (and folders). If you see a Confirm File Delete

box warning that a particular file is read-only, click **Yes** to continue. Also, you may see an error box warning that a specific file cannot be deleted because its path is unknown (or some other error), click **OK** to continue.

9. In the left pane, click **Change file name or keywords**.
10. Enter ***.tmp** in the left pane and click the **Search** button at the bottom of the pane.
11. After the search is completed, review the items on the list (see Figure 2-2). Press **Ctrl+A** to select all of the items found in the search. Press the **Del** key and click **Yes** to delete these temporary files (and folders).
12. Close the Search Results window.

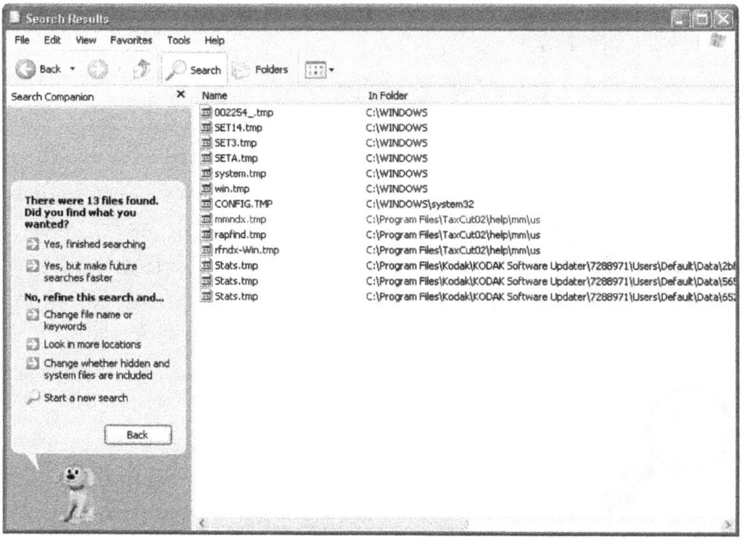

Figure 2-2: Results from the search for files ending with .tmp

Delete Temporary Files in Internet Explorer

As a Windows XP user, you probably also use Internet Explorer as your Web browser. When you browse the Web, lots of temporary files and cookies are left on your hard drive. The more you browse, the more temporary files are written to your computer. The temporary files may be pointers to Web pages, graphics, icons, and other types of files. Cookies are files that a Web server writes to your computer. The next time you access the Web site of that Web server, your computer transmits the cookie to the server. The cookie provides information about you, such as your name, preferences, interests, and so on. If you access a particular Web site often, a cookie for that Web site can make your access easier. However, there are many Web sites you never go back to and so cookies for these Web sites just take up space on your computer.

It is good practice to regularly delete temporary files. Also, plan to remove cookies from Web sites you do not typically access. One of the easiest ways to delete these files is by using the tools in Internet Explorer, as follows:

1. Open Internet Explorer, such as by clicking **Start** and then clicking **Internet** (or by double-clicking an Internet Explorer icon on your desktop).
2. Click the **Tools** menu and select **Internet Options**.
3. Ensure that the **General** tab is displayed.
4. You can view the temporary files saved by Internet Explorer to get an idea of the large numbers of temporary files and cookies. Click the **Settings** button in the middle section of the dialog box which is labeled Temporary Internet files (see

Figure 2-3). (If you are using Internet Explorer version 7, click the **Settings** button under Browsing history.) Click the **View Files** button. Scroll through the files to view them. Notice the cookies and consider whether you want to delete these. You can delete specific cookies by clicking them and pressing **Del** (or select multiple cookies to delete by holding down **Ctrl** and clicking the files, then press **Del**). If you see a Warning box, click **Yes** to confirm you want to delete the cookies. Close the Temporary Internet Files window. Click **Cancel** in the Settings dialog box.

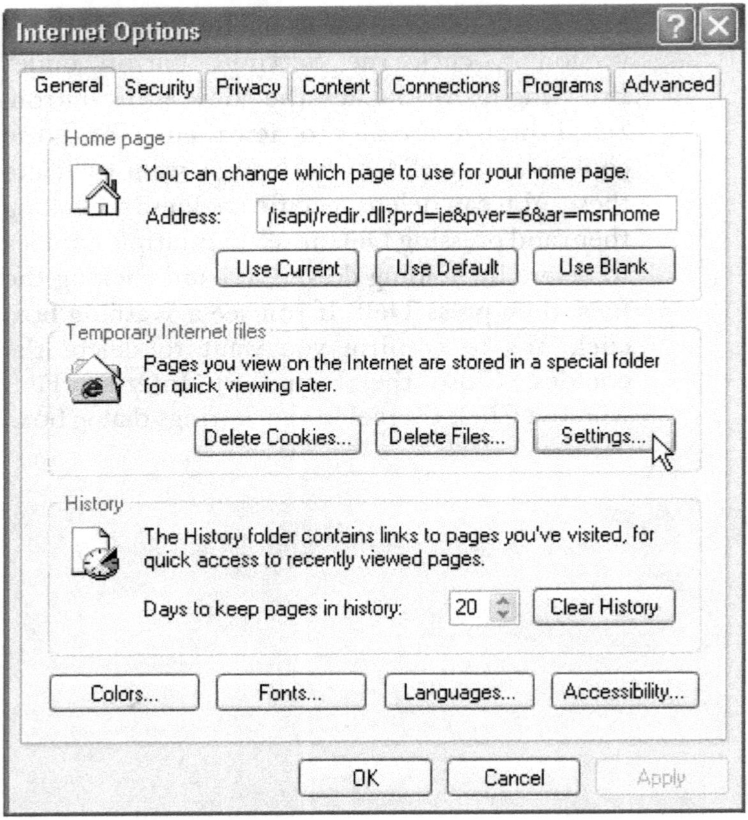

Figure 2-3: Clicking the Settings button

5. On the Internet Options box, click the **Delete Files** button. (If you are using Internet Explorer version 7, click the **Delete** button to delete temporary files, cookies, and other saved information; and skip to Step 9).

6. On the Delete Files dialog box, click the **Delete all offline content** box to place a check in it. Click **OK**.
7. Wait a few minutes while your temporary files are deleted.
8. If after viewing the cookie files in Step 4, and you've decided you can delete them all, click the **Delete Cookies** button. Click **OK**.
9. Close the Internet Options dialog box.
10. Close Internet Explorer.

Use Disk Cleanup

Windows XP (and other Windows versions) includes a utility called Disk Cleanup. This utility offers an additional way to clean up your hard drive for better performance. With Disk Cleanup, you can delete (see Figure 2-4):

- Downloaded program files
- Temporary Internet files
- Offline Web pages (depending on its setup, your computer may not include Offline Web pages)
- Microsoft Office setup files
- Recycle Bin files
- Setup log files
- Temporary files
- WebClient/Publisher temporary files
- Offline Files (depending on how it is set up, your computer may not include Offline Files and Temporary Offline Files)
- Temporary Offline Files

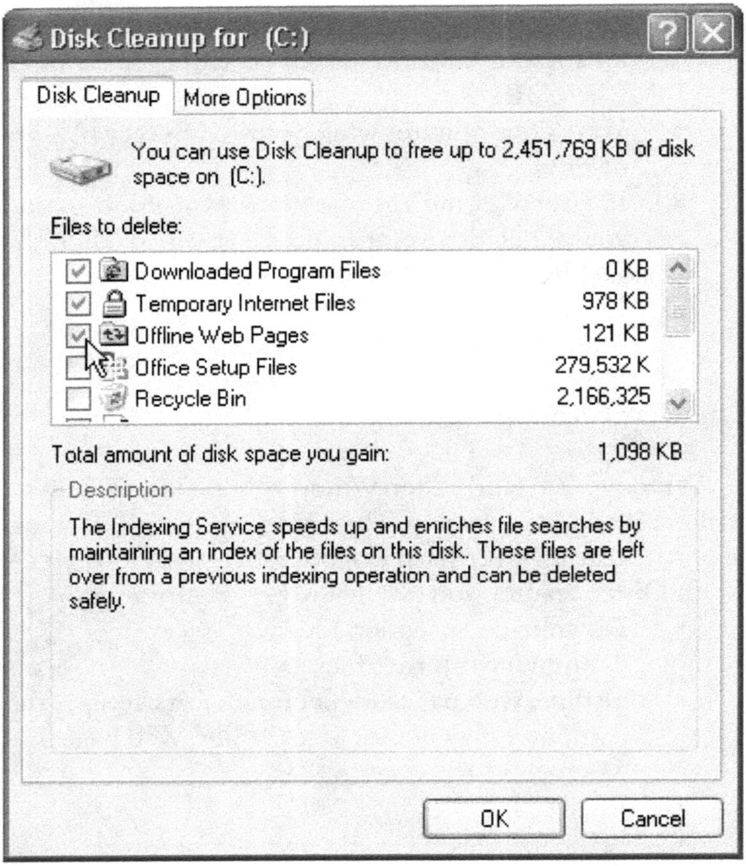

Figure 2-4: Disk Cleanup options

In addition to deleting these files, you can select to compress old files that have not been accessed for some time, which is the option *Compress old files*. Also, you can select to index files so they are located faster during searches, which is the option *Catalog files for the Content Indexer*.

It's usually a good idea to select all categories of files to delete. These are files you no longer need. One exception is the Recycle Bin which may still contain files you would like to undelete. (You can manage the Recycle Bin by double-clicking it on the desktop and may wish to delete files in this way instead of through Disk Cleanup.)

When you select the option *Compress old files*, Disk Cleanup uses the file compression utility in Windows XP to compress files you have not accessed for some time. Compressing files does not delete them or prevent you from accessing them. However, accessing the compressed files will be a little slower while they decompress. Also, compressed files cannot be indexed.

Selecting the *Catalog files for the Content Indexer* option is like a two-sided coin. The benefit is that files are indexed so that a file search works faster when you are trying to find a file, such as in My Computer. The downside is that your computer must initialize indexing each time you boot, which means that enabling indexing increases the startup time.

Use the following steps to access Disk Cleanup:

1. Click **Start**, click **All Programs**, click **Accessories**, click **System Tools**, and click **Disk Cleanup**. An alternative is to click **Start**, click **My Computer**, right-click **Local Disk (C:)**, click **Properties**, and click the **Disk Cleanup** button.
2. Disk Cleanup calculates the space that could be saved by using Disk Cleanup (see Figure 2-5). This can take a few minutes.

3. Select the deletion and other options of your choice (refer to Figure 2-4). For best performance of your computer, it is recommended that you select all of the deletion options (all options in the list from Downloaded Program Files through WebClient/Publisher Temporary Files to Temporary Offline Files).
4. Click **OK**.
5. Click **Yes**.

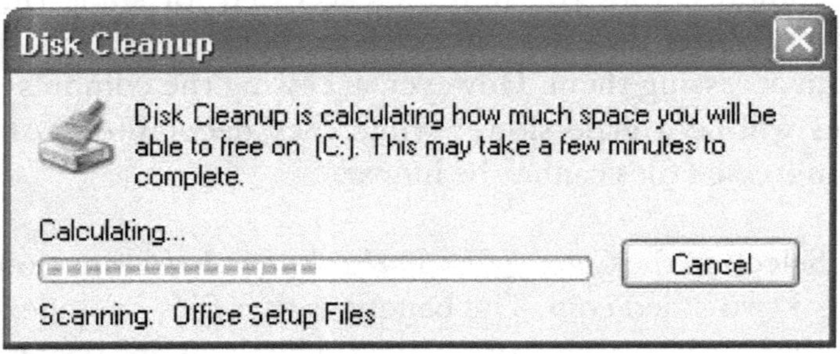

Figure 2-5: Disk Cleanup calculating space that can be freed

Running Programs Faster

Most of your time on a computer is spent running programs. Time spent waiting for a program to respond or to perform a specific action is wasted time. If you take a few moments to tune your computer, you'll spend less time waiting. Here are some actions you can take to help your programs run faster:

- Have the processor focus on running programs
- Ensure memory is set to stress running programs
- Configure a paging file

- Speed up the use of a paging file
- Remove programs you don't use

You learn how to perform these steps in the next sections.

Have the Processor Focus on Running Programs

Microsoft Windows operating systems, including Windows XP, come with program performance tuning options you can manage from Control Panel. An important option you can configure is the ability to have the central processing unit (CPU) devote most of its time to programs.

The steps for tuning the processor use are as follows:

1. Click **Start** and click **Control Panel**.
2. In the left pane of Control Panel, if you see *Switch to Classic View* then you are in the Category View of the Control Panel tool—stay in this view and click the **Performance and Maintenance** category, then click the **System** icon. If instead you see *Switch to Category View* in the left pane of Control Panel—stay in this view and double-click the **System** icon.
3. Click the **Advanced** tab in the System Properties dialog box.
4. Click the **Settings** button at the top, which is in the Performance area (see Figure 2-6).

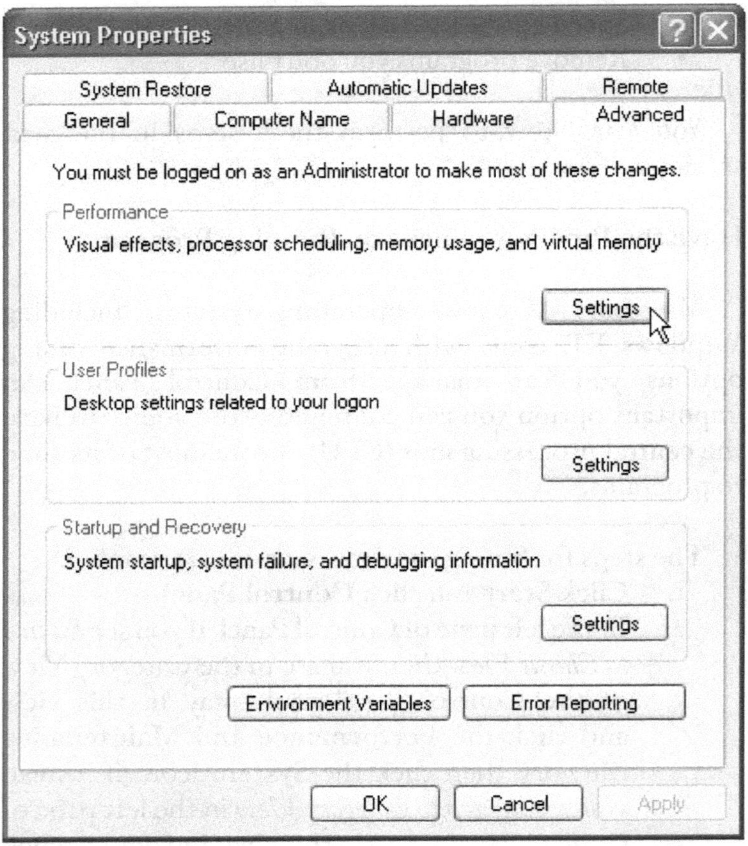

Figure 2-6: Selecting the Settings button for Performance

5. Click the **Advanced** tab in the Performance Options dialog box.
6. In the *Processor scheduling* area of the Advanced tab, ensure that **Programs** is selected (see Figure 2-7). This selection gives most processor time

to the program that is currently active (in the foreground), instead of to programs, services, and processes that may be running in the background.

7. Leave the Advanced tab open for your next tweak.

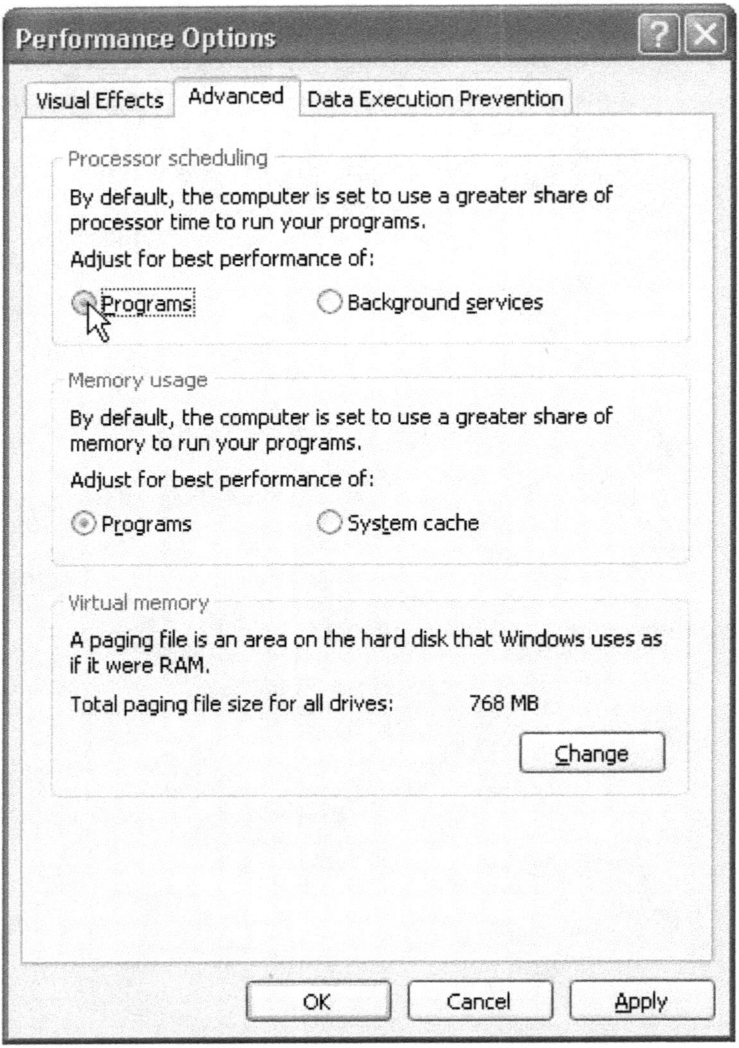

Figure 2-7: Selecting Programs for the processor performance setting

Ensure Memory is Used for Running Programs

While you have the Performance Options dialog box open, make sure that memory is set for running programs. The memory on your computer can be set up to mainly hold currently running programs. The other way to set memory is to have it mainly hold system cache, which is memory used for general system processes including network connection activities and system actions that run in the background. Generally, the only time when you would have memory set for system cache is if you use your Windows XP computer as a file server for network users rather than as your personal workstation. This might be the situation in a small business where employees access one Windows XP computer over the network as a server to their desktop computers.

To ensure your computer's memory is set to devote memory primarily to programs:

1. Make sure the **Advanced** tab is still available in the Performance Options dialog box (see the steps in the previous section).
2. Select **Programs** (if it is not already selected) in the *Memory usage* portion of the Advanced tab (Memory usage is the next section just under Processor scheduling, which you configured in Step 6 of the last set of steps).
3. Leave the Advanced tab open for one more tweak in the next section.

Configure a Paging File

The work your computer performs is done in two important memory locations: random access memory

(RAM) and virtual memory. When you think of RAM, think of the memory chips in your computer. This is the fastest memory available when you are working on your computer. However, there are many times when your computer has more work activities than can be stored in RAM. For these times, the spillover work is stored in a special area of the hard disk called virtual memory. Virtual memory is held in a file, called the paging file. As vacant space becomes available in RAM, portions of the paging file are transferred to RAM. Exchanges between RAM and the paging file are called paging and go on all of the time.

There are two things you should know about virtual memory. One is that its paging file can be too small, which causes delays when you are using programs and other computer features. The other is that virtual memory is not as fast as RAM, because pulling information from the hard disk is not as fast as pulling it from a memory chip.

If you want a fast computer, buy as much memory (RAM) as you can afford. This is as important as having a fast processor. But before you purchase more memory for a computer you already have, first try expanding the size of your paging file—which is free, easy to do, and an immediate solution.

Tip: If you are not sure how much memory is in your computer click Start, click My Computer, and click View system information in the left pane (under System Tasks). On the General tab under the Computer category, look for xxx MB of RAM or xx GB of RAM.

Here's how to configure the paging file:

1. Ensure the **Advanced** tab is still available in the Performance Options dialog box (see the steps in the previous two sections). If it is closed, click **Start**, click **Control Panel**, click **Performance and Maintenance** (only if you are in the Category View of Control Panel), click **System**, click the **Advanced** tab, click the **Settings** button under Performance, and click the **Advanced** tab.
2. Click the **Change** button in the Virtual memory area of the Performance Options dialog box.
3. As you configure the paging file, consider the following tips:
   - Configure a paging file on each disk volume. For example, if you have a computer with two hard disks, make sure there as a paging file on both disks (such as Drive C: and Drive D:).
   - Ensure that the initial size of a paging file is at least 2.5 times the amount of RAM in your computer. For instance, if your computer has 512 MB of RAM, then configure the initial size of the paging file to be 512 x 2.5 = 1280 MB. Table 2-1 illustrates common configurations.
   - Set the maximum size for the paging file to be two times or more that of the initial size. If your computer's response is slow, consider making the maximum size three times the initial size (see Table 2-1). For example, if your computer has an initial size of 1280 MB, make the maximum size at least 1280 x 2 =

2560 MB. Or if your computer has seemed extra slow, make the maximum size 1280 x 3 = 3840 MB or higher.

- Another strategy preferred by some computer professionals is to set the initial and maximum paging file sizes the same, so that your computer does not take extra time in expanding the size of the paging file, when this is needed for large applications. For example, if you have 512 MB of RAM, you might set both the initial and maximum paging file sizes at 2560 MB.

4. Click the drive you want to configure, such as **C:**.
5. Click the option button for **Custom size:**, if it is not already selected.
6. Enter the value you've calculated for the **Initial size (MB):**, such as **1280** MB for a computer that has 512 MB of RAM.
7. Enter the **Maximum size (MB):** that you calculated, such as **2560** or **3840** MB for a computer that has 512 MB of RAM and a paging file with an initial size of 1280 MB.
8. Click the **Set** button (see Figure 2-8).

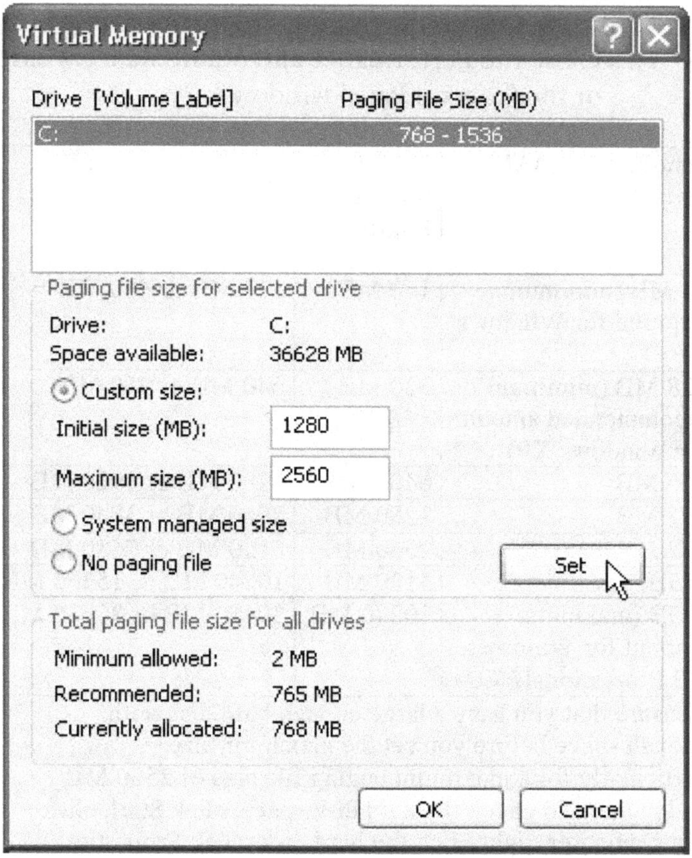

Figure 2-8: Configuring the paging file

9. If the Drive [Volume Label] listing at the top of the Virtual Memory dialog box lists other drives, click each drive one at a time and repeat Steps 5—8.
10. Click **OK** on the Virtual Memory dialog box.
11. Click **OK** on the Performance Options dialog box.

12. Click **OK** on the System Properties dialog box.
13. Close the Performance and Maintenance window or the Control Panel window.

Amount of RAM in Your Computer	Initial Size of Paging File	Maximum Size of Paging File*
64 MB (minimum required for Windows XP)	160 MB	320 MB or 480 MB
128 MB (minimum recommended amount for Windows XP)	320 MB	640 MB or 960 MB
256 MB	640 MB	1280 MB or 1920 MB
512 MB	1280 MB	2560 MB or 3840 MB
1 GB	2560 MB	5120 MB or 7680 MB
2 GB	5120 MB	10240 MB or 15360 MB
4 GB (maximum amount for Windows XP Professional)	10240 MB	20480 MB or 30720 MB

*Ensure that you have a large enough hard disk with enough space before you set the maximum size, particularly for a maximum paging file size of 2560 MB and higher. To check the hard disk space, click Start, click My Computer, right-click the hard disk, click Properties, and display the General tab.

Table 2-1: Paging File Sizes

Speed Up the Paging File

Many computers have over 256 MB of RAM. If your computer has more RAM, such as 512 MB or more, you can improve paging file performance by ensuring that as much RAM as possible is used prior to spilling over data from RAM to the paging file. (Remember RAM is faster than virtual memory because it's on chips.) Here are some simple steps you can take to accomplish this:

1. Click **Start**.
2. Click **Run**.
3. Type **msconfig** and click **OK**.
4. Click the **SYSTEM.INI** tab. (system.ini is a file your computer uses at startup.)
5. Click the **plus sign** in front of **[386enh]** to show the items under it.
6. Click the last item listing under [386enh], such as CGA40WOA.FON=CGA40WOA.FON (the last item listed may have a different name on your computer, depending on your configuration).
7. Click the **New** button and enter, **Conservativ eSwapfileUsage=1** (do not put spaces before or after the equal sign).
8. Click **OK**.
9. Close all open programs and windows and then click **Restart** in the System Configuration box.
10. Log on after your system reboots.
11. Click the box for **Don't show this message or launch the System Configuration Utility when Windows starts**.
12. Click **OK**.

Another strategy to speed up the paging file is to regularly defragment the file so the contents of the paging file are all right next to each other on the same area of the disk. This makes it faster for your hard disk to find information in the paging file. One way to defragment the paging file is to:

1. Delete the paging file (use the steps described in the "Configure a Paging File" section, but instead of sizing the file, select **No paging file**—refer to Figure 2-8). You have to delete the file because the defragmenting software in Windows XP does not defragment the paging file, since it is always open.
2. Defragment the disk used for the paging file (see Chapter 3 to learn how to defragment a disk).
3. Recreate the paging file (use the steps described in the "Configure a Paging File" section).

Remove Programs You Don't Use

You can help your system run more efficiently when you get rid of programs you don't use. Removing these programs returns valuable disk space and gets rid of old program components that may conflict with those used by newer programs and program versions. This process is the computer equivalent of cleaning out your garage and getting rid of all the junk you don't use anymore, so you can more easily find the tools and lawn implements you use all of the time, as well as to be able to drive your car into the garage without hitting anything.

Try these steps to remove programs you don't use:

1. Click **Start**.
2. Click **Control Panel**.
3. Click or double-click (depending on whether you are in Control Panel's Category or Classic View) **Add or Remove Programs**.

4. Review the list of programs.
5. When you find a program you don't use (be absolutely certain you don't use it), click that program.
6. Click the **Remove** or **Change/Remove** button (the type of button displayed depends on the program) and follow the instructions for removing that particular program (see Figure 2-9).
7. Repeat Steps 4 through 6 for each program you want to remove.
8. Close the Add or Remove Programs window when you are finished removing programs.
9. Close the Control Panel window.

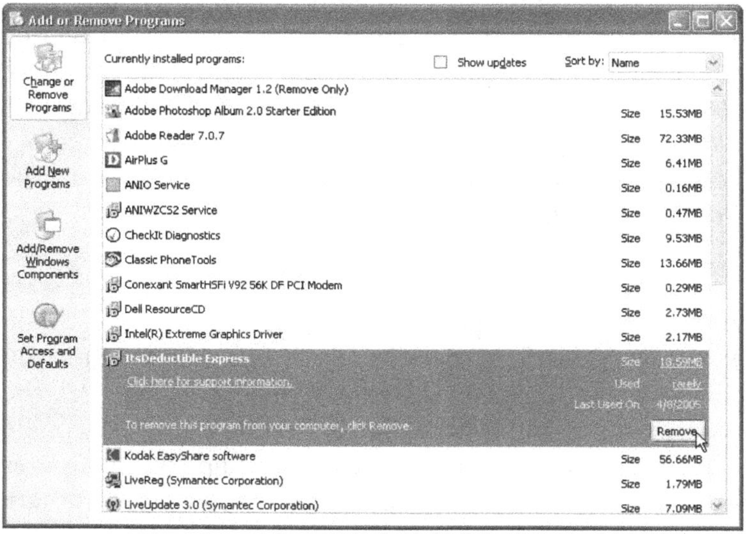

Figure 2-9: Removing a program

Taming Windows Prefetch Capability

Windows XP tries to anticipate your needs as a way to speed up program access. It does this through the prefetch capability. When you start an application, such as e-mail, Windows XP adds information about it to the Prefetch folder. The next time your computer is started, the contents of the Prefetch folder are reviewed. While reviewing the Prefetch folder, Windows XP loads into memory portions of applications you have recently run, so the applications start faster the next time you select to run them.

The plus side of prefetch is that applications start faster. The minus side is that as more applications are added to the Prefetch folder your computer's startup time may be slower, because it takes longer for the computer to examine the Prefetch folder and then load all of the program elements it finds. Also, the computer's performance as you're working is likely to be slowed, because its memory is already packed with the program elements loaded via the Prefetch folder.

The bottom line is that your computer is likely to start and run faster if you periodically delete the contents of the Prefetch folder. This gives it a fresh start. Right after you clean out the folder, Windows XP begins adding back the programs you run. If you clean out the folder every couple of weeks or every month, you can speed up your computer and ensure that only the most recently used programs are known to prefetch.

You can clean out the Prefetch folder by using these steps:

1. Click **Start**.
2. Click **My Computer**.
3. Double-click the disk that contains your Windows folder, which is most likely to be **Local Disk (C:)**.
4. Double-click the **WINDOWS** folder. If the WINDOWS screen has a message about the files being hidden, click **Show the contents of this folder**.
5. Double-click the **Prefetch** folder (you'll need to scroll to find it).
6. Press **Ctrl+A** (or click the **Edit** menu and click **Select All**).
7. Press the **Del** key.
8. Click **Yes**. (If you get an Error Deleting File or Folder message, note the name of the file that cannot be deleted and click **OK**. Typically files that begin with RUNDLL32 or LAUNCH are currently open and cannot be deleted—but there are others that may be open, too. Next, hold down the **Ctrl** key and click all other files, omitting the one(s) that cannot be deleted. Press **Del** and click **Yes**.)
9. Close the Prefetch folder.

If there are certain programs that you always want to have prefetch capability so they load quickly, you can have those programs add their information to the Prefetch folder when you run them. Here's how:

1. Find a shortcut that runs the program, such as a shortcut icon on the desktop. A shortcut icon has

a black arrow in a white box on the lower left side of the icon.

2. Right-click the program's shortcut icon and click **Properties**.
3. Click the **Shortcut** tab.
4. Find the Target: box and notice the contents. This is the information about where to find the program and to start it. At the end of the line (outside of the ending double quote mark), type one blank space and then type in **/prefetch:1**. (Some programs, such as Microsoft Office programs, do not allow you to change the information in the Target box.)
5. Click **OK** (see Figure 2-10).
6. Start the program to ensure it will start. In a small number of cases the program may start with an error message because it is incompatible with the prefetch directive. If so, simply go through Steps 1 through 5, but remove the /prefetch:1 directive you added.

Tip: You can create a shortcut by using My Computer to find the program, which is typically in a subfolder under the Program Files folder and has the .exe extension plus the program's icon. Right-click the icon and click Create Shortcut. This creates a shortcut icon for the program. If you want to have your new shortcut icon on the desktop, drag it to the desktop. You can delete a shortcut at any time by right clicking it, clicking Delete, and clicking Delete Shortcut.

Figure 2-10: Adding the prefetch directive to start a program faster

Updating Your System Painlessly

Microsoft regularly issues updates to Windows XP. The updates may fix problems that cause your computer to run more slowly or that may even interrupt normal functioning. There are also updates to improve security. Most updates don't take much time to download and install. Occasionally, Microsoft issues a Service Pack, which is a major update that can take more time to perform than regular updates.

To keep your computer on the fast track and running smoothly, plan to install new updates. Microsoft Windows Update is a tool that examines your computer and determines which updates need to be performed. One approach is to run Windows Update manually every week or two weeks. Another approach is to have Windows XP automatically run Windows Update on a regular schedule that you determine. Windows Update can run in the background so you hardly notice. To run Windows Update you need to be connected to the Internet so that you can access Microsoft's Windows Update Web site.

The steps for running Windows Update manually are:

1. Click **Start**.
2. Point to **All Programs**.
3. Click **Windows Update**.
4. Your computer may be examined by the Windows Update Web site to determine if it has the latest updating software. For example, Microsoft now offers Microsoft Update, which enables you to obtain updates in one place for Windows XP and other Microsoft products such as Microsoft Office. If you have other Microsoft products,

consider following the directions to install Microsoft Update. If necessary, click **Start now** again from the Microsoft Update Web site. Review the license agreement and click **Continue**. If requested, click the bar just below the address bar on your browser to install ActiveX controls. After Microsoft Update is installed, if necessary, click **Check for Updates** to find updates your computer needs.

5. No matter whether you are using Windows Update or Microsoft Update, click the **Express** button to install "high-priority updates."
6. The Web site will check your computer for updates that have not been installed. Follow the instructions to load the updates you want.

Here's how you can set up Windows Update to run automatically:

1. Click **Start**.
2. Right-click **My Computer**.
3. Click **Properties**.
4. Click the **Automatic Updates** tab in the System Properties dialog box.
5. Click **Automatic (recommended)**.
6. Select the interval to automatically check for updates, such as **Every Wednesday** at **12:00 PM** (see Figure 2-11).
7. Click **OK**.

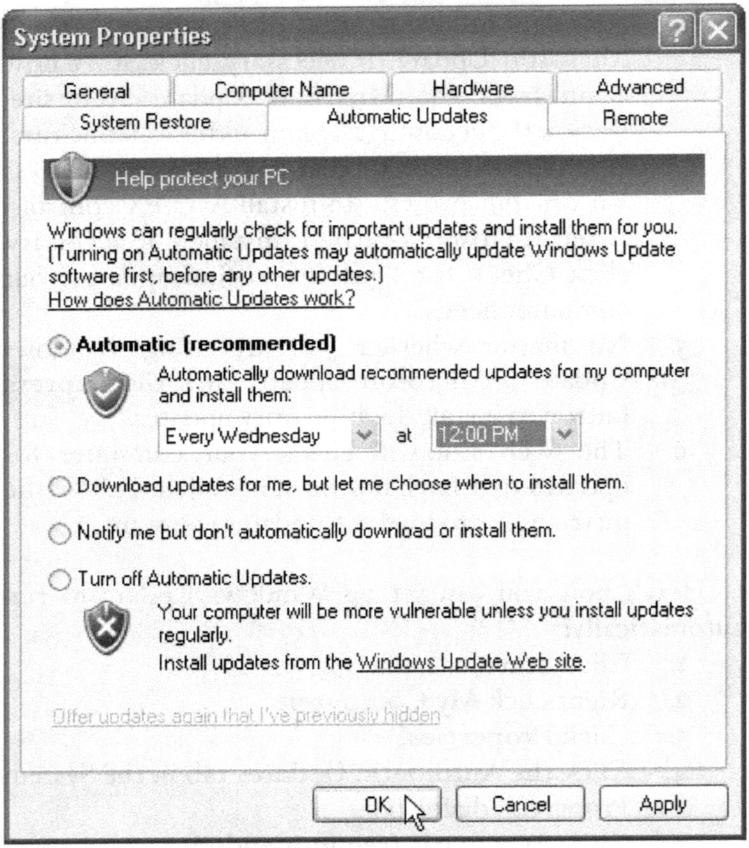

Figure 2-11: Configuring automatic updating

Tips for Those Who Want to Work with the Registry

The Registry contains settings that you can configure to help your computer run faster. Four very useful Registry changes can help to speed up:

- Folder access
- Menu display
- Applications
- The operating system

The following sections show you how to make these Registry changes.

Access Folders Faster

No matter whether you are inside a program, such as Microsoft Word or using My Computer, you want a snappy response when you are navigating through folders to open a specific file. This is particularly true when there are many subdirectories to go through. You can speed up access to folders by telling Windows XP to stop recording the date when each folder was last accessed. Normally, even if you only open a folder to view its contents, Windows XP changes the last accessed date.

The Registry modification for this tweak is as follows:

1. Click **Start**.
2. Click **Run**.
3. Enter **regedit** and click **OK**.
4. Open (or double-click) the **HKEY_LOCAL_MACHINE** folder in the left pane. (Note that the regedit program remembers which folders you have opened in the past, so that some of the folders mentioned in these steps may be open already.)
5. Open the **SYSTEM** folder in the left pane.
6. Open the **CurrentControlSet** folder in the left pane.

7. Open the **Control** folder in the left pane.
8. Click the **Edit** menu.
9. Click **New**.
10. Click **DWORD value**.
11. Type in a new value of **NtfsDisableLastAccessU pdate** and press **Enter**.
12. Double-click **NtfsDisableLastAccessUpdate**.
13. Enter 1 in the **Value data:** box and click **OK**.
14. Close the Registry Editor window.
15. Your change will take effect after you restart your computer, which you do now or you can restart after you complete all of the steps in this section. If you select to restart now, close all open windows and programs. Click **Start**, click **Turn Off Computer** and click **Restart**. (If you are using Windows XP without certain updates your shutdown procedure may be to click **Start**, click **Shut Down**, select **Restart**, and click **OK**.)

Display Menus Faster

If you like your Windows desktop menus to display faster, give the following Registry change a try:

1. Click **Start**.
2. Click **Run**.
3. Enter **regedit** and click **OK**.
4. Open (double-click) the **HKEY_CURRENT_ USER** folder in the left pane.
5. Open the **Control Panel** folder in the left pane.
6. Open the **Desktop** folder in the left pane.
7. Double-click **MenuShowDelay** in the right pane. The default setting is likely to be at 400. You can speed up the display by lowering the setting to

50. Enter **50** in the **Value data:** box. Click **OK.** (Note, you can go back and change the value higher than 50 or lower to match your preference. The change, though, will not go into effect until you restart the computer.)
8. Close the Registry Editor window.
9. Restart your computer.

Speed Up Applications

Every application that you run in Windows XP is given a priority. The more priority an application has, the more processor time it is given in comparison to other programs on the computer. You can speed up applications you are currently using by having Windows XP give those applications a higher priority and having each program's window run in its own location in memory. Besides speed, another advantage is that programs will run more stably. The disadvantage is that programs running in the background, such as printing, will likely run a little slower. If you are willing to accept this tradeoff, consider the following Registry modification:

1. Click **Start**.
2. Click **Run**.
3. Enter **regedit** and click **OK**.
4. Open (double-click) the **HKEY_LOCAL_MACHINE** folder in the left pane.
5. Open the **SYSTEM** folder in the left pane.
6. Open the **CurrentControlSet** folder in the left pane.
7. Open the **Control** folder in the left pane.
8. Open the **PriorityControl** folder in the left pane.

9. Double-click **Win32PrioritySeparation** in the right pane.
10. Change the **Value data:** setting to **38** (from the default of 2) and click **OK**.
11. Close the Registry Editor window.
12. Click **Start**.
13. Click **My Computer**.
14. Click the **Tools** menu.
15. Click **Folder Options**.
16. Click the **View** tab.
17. Check **Launch folder windows in a separate process**.
18. Click **OK**.
19. Restart your computer.

If you are unsure about making this Registry change, you can manually give a specific application more priority than others. You might do this, for example, if you are working to make a deadline to finish a document or spreadsheet. To increase the priority of a specific application, such as Microsoft Word or Excel:

1. Right-click the taskbar in an open area (not on a button or icon) and click **Task Manager**.
2. Ensure the **Applications** tab is showing.
3. Find the application that you want to run faster.
4. Right-click the application and click **Go To Process**. This action takes you to the Processes tab and highlights the process your application is running.
5. Right-click the highlighted process and point to **Set Priority**.

6. Click **AboveNormal** or **High**. DO NOT CLICK Realtime. (Realtime gives too much processor time to the application so your computer won't be able to do much else).
7. Click **Yes** in the warning window.
8. Close the Windows Task Manager window. The priority setting you have established will last for as long as you stay in the application, but will not be in effect after you close the application and start it later.

Lock the Operating System Files in RAM for Faster Response

If your computer has 512 MB or more of RAM, consider setting Windows XP so that the main operating system program code (called the kernel) is always retained in RAM and not moved into the paging file. Doing this helps your computer run faster because so many of the actions you perform on the computer involve the operating system program code. Similar to other programs, the operating system code runs faster when it operates out or RAM instead of out of the paging file.

Use these steps to ensure the operating system program code operates from RAM:

1. Click **Start**.
2. Click **Run**.
3. Enter **regedit** and click **OK**.
4. Open the **HKEY_LOCAL_MACHINE** folder in the left pane.
5. Open the **SYSTEM** folder in the left pane.
6. Open the **CurrentControlSet** folder in the left pane.

7. Open the **Control** folder in the left pane.
8. Open the **Session Manager** folder in the left pane.
9. Open the **Memory Management** folder in the left pane.
10. Double-click **DisablePagingExecutive** in the right pane.
11. Enter **1** for the **Value data:** and click **OK**.
12. Close the Registry Editor window.
13. Restart the computer.

Chapter 3

Speed Up Your Disks

Your computer's hard disks are a vast warehouse of storage for all the programs and files on your computer. Just about every time you access a file or open a program, you access a hard disk, so speeding up disk access is a great way to expedite your whole computing experience. In this chapter you learn a variety of methods to tune disks for speed, about fast external disk access, and how to make simple Registry changes for faster disk access.

Tuning Disks

Tuning your disks can yield important results for speedy access to the information stored on them. Just as you need to periodically tune your car, you should plan to do the same thing for the disks on your computer. Tuning an auto often results in faster response plus better gas mileage. Tuning your computer's disks can yield faster information access and prolong the life of your disks.

Plan to take the following actions to improve disk speed and reliability:

- Set the disks in DMA mode
- Defragment the disks
- Manage the Recycle Bin
- Compress large files
- Plan your file names

You learn how to take these actions in the next sections.

Set Your Disks in DMA Mode

A simple but important step you can take to ensure your hard disk access is fast is to use the fastest method for transferring information from disk to memory. Most desktop computers have Integrated Device Electronics (IDE) drives. A main characteristic of this kind of drive is that the circuit board (card) used to manage the drive is on the drive itself, instead of being a separate card plugged into a slot inside your computer. IDE drives use either of two transfer methods: Program Input/Output (PIO) and Direct Memory Access (DMA).

The PIO data transfer method uses two steps when you access information on your disk. Step one is to transfer a portion of the information into a CPU storage area that uses "registers." Registers are high-speed memory on the CPU that the CPU uses in its processing activities. From the registers, the information is transferred into regular memory (RAM) by the CPU so you can use the information. Going through the CPU memory slows down both the access to information on the drive and the response of your computer. Another problem is that the information transfer takes twice as long because it goes through one kind of memory (the CPU memory) and then another kind of memory (the RAM). In human terms, this is like repeating everything you say twice.

You can bypass using the CPU memory by implementing the DMA transfer method. The DMA data transfer method uses only one step, which is to transfer the information you access directly into memory from the disk. DMA is faster than PIO for data transfers because there is no waiting on the CPU to move information into and out of its registers. Further, DMA boosts the speed of the computer because the CPU is not distracted from other processing while it manages data sent to and from a disk drive.

Use the following steps to ensure your computer is set to use the DMA data transfer method:

Tip: For the best results, close any open windows or active programs before you start the steps presented in this chapter.

1. Click **Start**.
2. Right-click **My Computer**.
3. Click **Manage**.
4. Click **Device Manager** in the left pane under System Tools.
5. Double-click **IDE ATA/ATAPI controllers** in the right pane.
6. Right-click **Primary IDE Channel**.
7. Click **Properties** (see Figure 3-1).

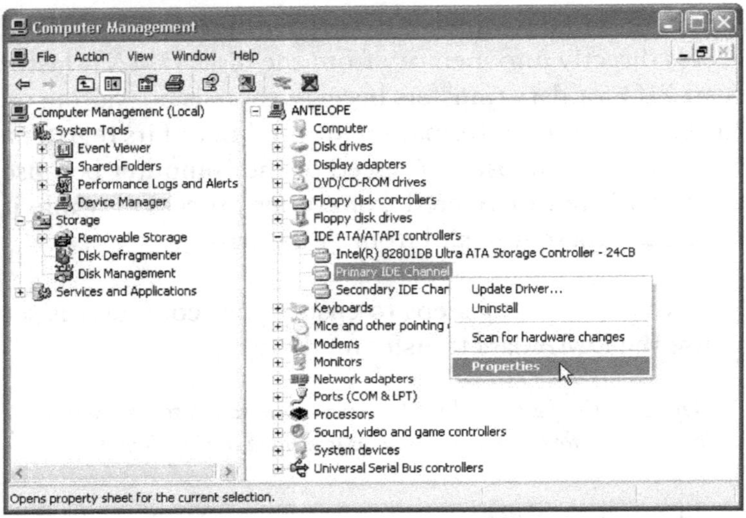

Figure 3-1: Configuring the Primary IDE Channel

8. Click the **Advanced Settings** tab.
9. For all devices listed, ensure that the Transfer Mode: box (or boxes for multiple devices) is set to **DMA if available.**
10. Click **OK.**
11. If you see Secondary IDE Channel under IDE ATA/ATAPI controllers in the right pane, right-click this option and click **Properties**. Repeat Steps 8 through 10.
12. Close the Computer Management window when you are finished.

Defragment Your Disks

As you create and delete files, the files get more and more spread out all over the disk. Portions of a single file may be located in several different places. At the same time, empty spaces develop throughout the disk as files are created, deleted, and modified. The scattering of files, portions of files, and empty pockets is called fragmentation.

Before long, fragmentation can slow disk operations because the read heads on your disk drive have to jump all over the place to locate specific files. In the days of mainframes with large disk cabinets, fragmentation could be severe enough that an entire cabinet would walk across the floor as the disk read heads went back and forth searching for files. Besides creating extra disk wear, fragmentation slows down your access to data.

File access is faster if each file is in one continuous location (not split up all over the disk), and there are no empty pockets between files. The process of rearranging files so they are contiguous (next to each other) and removing empty spaces is called defragmentation or defragging. Windows XP has a disk defragmentation tool that can speed up your disks and prolong their life. Plan to use the tool at least once a month.

Use the following steps to defragment a disk:

1. Choose a time, such as in the evening, when you don't need to use the computer for half an hour or so. Also, make sure you've closed all programs and open windows. (This is also an opportunity to defrag the space occupied by your paging file as mentioned in Chapter 2 under the section, "Speed Up the Paging File.")
2. Click **Start**.

3. Point to **All Programs**.
4. Point to **Accessories**.
5. Point to **System Tools**.
6. Click **Disk Defragmenter**. (Another way to start Disk Defragmenter is to click Start, click My Computer, right-click the disk you want to defragment, click Properties, click the Tools tab, and click the Defragment Now button.)
7. At this point you can choose to analyze a disk to see if it needs to be defragmented or you can immediately start the defragmentation process. It is recommended that you go ahead and defragment the disk to ensure you have done what you can to reduce the disk's work load and increase its speed.
8. Ensure that the disk you want to defragment is selected under the Volume category near the top of the window.
9. Click the **Defragment** button (see Figure 3-2).

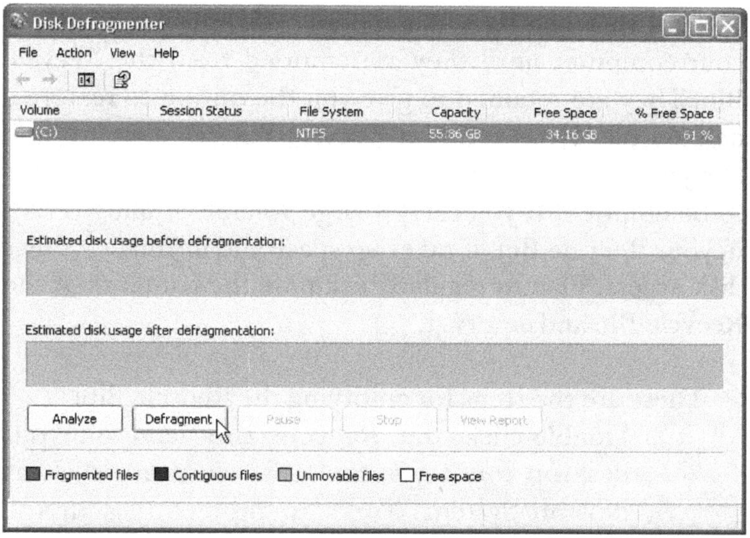

Figure 3-2: Defragmenting a disk

10. The information line at the bottom of the Disk Defragmenter window shows the progress of defragmentation.
11. After the defragmentation process is finished, click **Close**.
12. Close the Disk Defragmenter window.

Manage the Recycle Bin

Another way to improve disk efficiency and to provide more disk space for your work is to actively manage your Recycle Bin. You can do this in two ways:

1. Regularly empty the Recycle Bin.
2. Reduce the size of the Recycle Bin.

Files that you have deleted are not fully purged from your computer until they are emptied from the Recycle Bin. They are retained to give you the option to restore a deleted file. However, that Recycle Bin can start to look like your trash can after you've hosted a big party: it needs to be emptied! If you carry a large volume of unused files in your Recycle Bin, it takes up space and ultimately slows disk access. Plan to regularly examine the contents of the Recycle Bin and empty it.

These are the steps for emptying the Recycle Bin:

1. Double-click the **Recycle Bin** icon on your desktop (or if you are using software such as Norton System Works to protect files in the Recycle Bin, right-click it and click **Open**).
2. Scroll through the contents to ensure there are no files you want to retain.
3. If you want to delete all of the files in the Recycle Bin, click the **File** menu and click **Empty Recycle Bin**. Click **Yes** to delete the files. If there are files you don't want to delete just now, press and hold the **Ctrl** key and then click each file that can be deleted. Press **Del** and click **Yes**.
4. Close the Recycle Bin window.

By default, the Recycle Bin occupies 10 percent of your hard disk. In most cases, that's a lot of unused space, particularly if you regularly empty the Recycle Bin. Consider resizing the Recycle Bin to much less, such as to 4 or 5 percent of the disk.

Use these steps to resize the Recycle Bin:

1. Right-click the **Recycle Bin** on the desktop and click **Properties**.
2. Click the **Global** tab, if it is not already selected.
3. Ensure that **Use one setting for all drives:** is selected.
4. Move the slider bar in the middle of the window to reach **5%** as shown in Figure 3-3, or 4% if you want to save even more room on your hard disk for other uses. (Note that the Recycle Bin in Figure 3-3 is protected by Norton SystemWorks.)
5. Click **OK**.

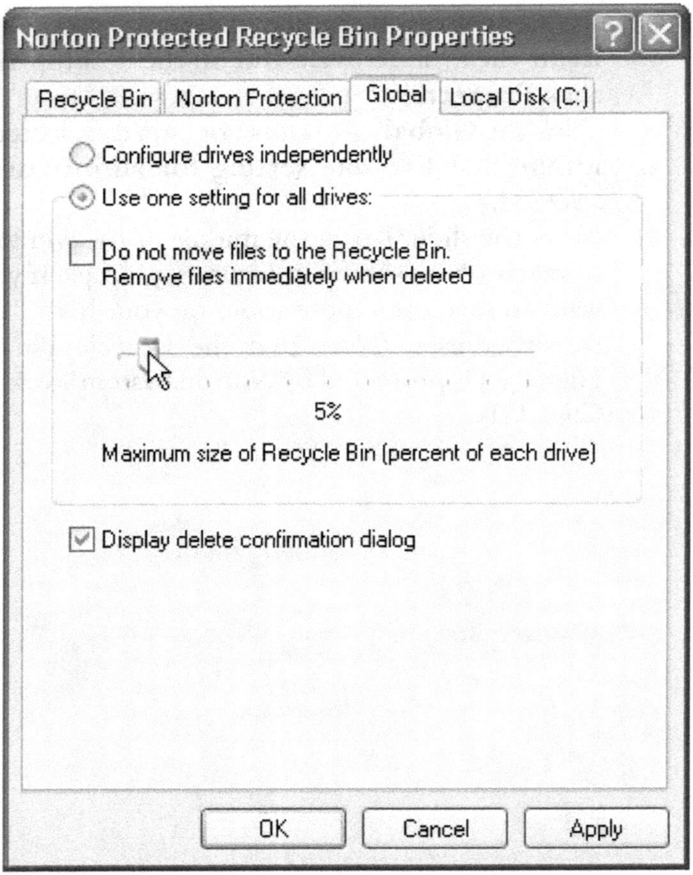

Figure 3-3: Setting the Recycle Bin to 5% of disk size

Fix Disk Problems

All the information on your hard disk is stored in tracks and sectors. A hard disk is a sealed unit that contains circular metallic platters. The platters are separated so that information can be written on both sides and written or read by read heads attached to "arms." Each side of each platter is divided into tracks and sectors. You might think of tracks as similar to rings in a tree trunk. Every track is divided into smaller units called sectors. Over time a particular track, sector, or both may experience wear or slight damage. These areas can create problems for reading or writing information. They also can delay the response of your computer.

Fortunately, you can find and fix problem sectors by using *chkdsk*, which you learned about in Chapter 1. You can also use the disk drive error-checking software in Windows XP, which enables you to initiate *chkdsk* and to specify if you want to fix errors in system files and fix bad sectors. Error checking a disk takes time and it requires sole use of the disk, which is why you have to restart your computer after you set up error checking to run. Consider running this process over lunch or in the evening when you are not using your computer. The steps to follow are:

1. Click **Start**.
2. Click **My Computer**.
3. Right-click the hard disk you want to check for errors, such as **Local Disk (C:)**.
4. Click **Properties**.
5. Click the **Tools** tab.
6. Click the **Check Now** button (see Figure 3-4, note that if you have Windows XP Professional you may see an additional option for backing up your disk, depending on how your system is configured—also if you have some types of disk management software such as from Norton, you may see an additional tab for that software).

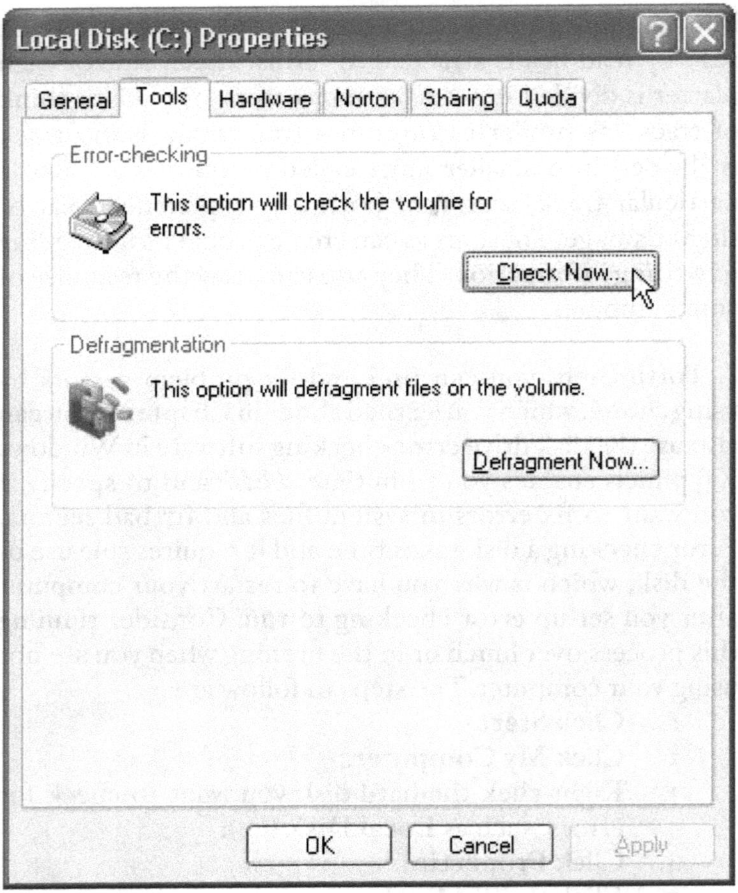

Figure 3-4: Checking a hard disk for errors in Windows XP Home Edition

7. Check the boxes for **Automatically fix file system errors** and **Scan for and attempt recovery of bad sectors.**
8. Click **Start.**

9. Click **Yes** to start the error scan the next time you restart your computer.
10. Close all open windows or applications and restart your computer.

Compress Large Files

Some types of files, such as files containing photographs, can occupy lots of disk space. One photograph file in .tif format, for example, may be 1 to 2 MB in size. It doesn't take long for a photograph collection to grow into hundreds of files. Also, because photograph files are large, they can take awhile to load.

Music files are another example of large files. Music files, such as in the .mp3 format, are often over 2 MB in size. Video and combined video/audio files are yet another source of large files. Still another source of large files is text/graphics files in the .pdf format for viewing in Adobe Reader.

You can take action to manage large files in the following ways:

- Regularly review your folders that contain large files and delete the files you don't need.
- Whenever possible compress large files. Compressing files reduces the amount of space needed to store them.
- Convert or compress photo files to formats that take less space.

Plan to use My Computer to open the folders that contain large files and then determine if there are files you can delete. For photo and video files, you may use software such as Adobe Photoshop or Kodak EasyShare, which provide tools for deleting photos or deleting entire albums of photos.

Windows XP includes the ability to compress files and folders. Also, you can purchase software that has multiple features for compressing files and folders. Examples of software that you can purchase are:

- CompreXX by MirmarSinan
- CVista PdfCompressor by CVision Technologies for compressing .pdf files used by Adobe Reader
- PKZip by PKWare
- Stuffit and ZipMagic by SmithMicro Software
- WinZip by WinZip

Tip: Before you compress your files, test the software out on a few files in a test folder to make sure the software still enables you to access the files in the way you want to use them.

If you plan to use the compression capability in Windows XP (again first test the files by using a small sampling in a test folder):

1. Click **Start**.
2. Click **My Computer**.
3. Locate the folder containing the files you want to compress; or locate a specific file to compress.
4. Right-click the folder or file and click **Properties**.
5. Ensure the **General** tab is displayed.
6. Click the **Advanced** button in the Attributes section of the dialog box.
7. Click **Compress contents to save disk space** (see Figure 3-5).

8. Click **OK**.
9. Click **OK** again. If you are compressing the contents of a folder, you may see the Confirm Attribute Changes box with options to apply the changes to only this folder or to the folder, its subfolders and files. Click the option, **Apply changes to this folder, subfolders and files** and then click **OK**.
10. Close My Computer.

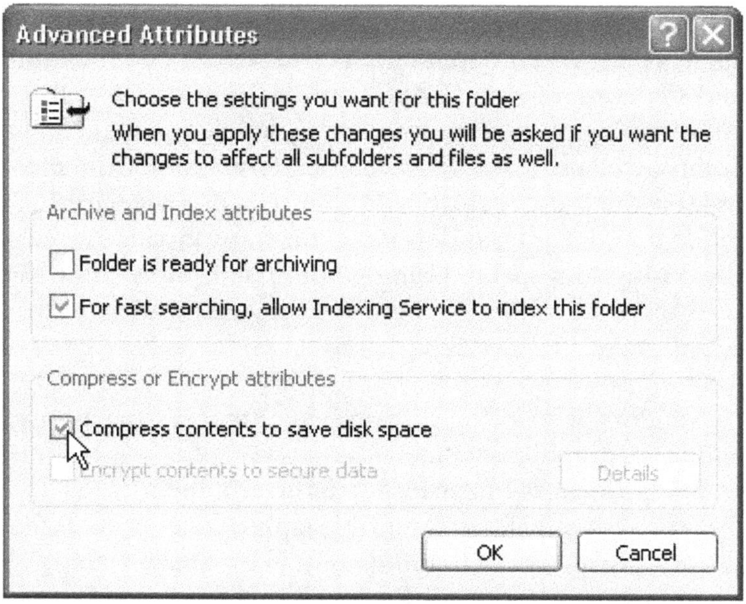

Figure 3-5: Compressing a folder in Windows XP

Often when you transfer a photo from your digital camera to your computer, it is saved in an uncompressed format, such as a .tif file. Other formats typically used for photos are .gif and .jpg. All of these file formats can be significantly compressed. For example, you might compress a photo in the .tif format from 1.25 MB to 128 KB, which is a significant savings in disk space and yields a photo that loads much faster from disk—and is faster to send over the Internet, such as through e-mail. If you have a lot of photos, consider purchasing software that can specifically compress or convert .tif, .gif, and .jpg files.

The .tif format can be compressed using methods such as LZW compression, HUFFMAN compression, and G3 compression. LZW compression works well for compressing photos without losing detail. .jpg files can be compressed using various levels of compression from most to least. .gif files are relatively compressed in the native .gif mode because .gif was developed for transporting graphics files using less space. Using compressed photo files can really save you a lot of time when they load and when you e-mail them.

Vendors who offer software for compressing photos and other graphics include:

- Convert Image by Softinterface, Inc.
- Graphic Converter by Graphic Converter
- ReaConverter and ReaJPEG by ReaSoft.com
- SnowBatch and RasterMaster from Snowbound Software

Plan Your File Names

Your computer's file system alphabetizes the file names inside a folder each time you access the folder using My

Computer. You can speed opening a folder, particularly if it contains lots of files with similar names, by planning how to name the files in advance. For example, consider the following series of files in the Financials folder:

Month End Spreadsheet January
Month End Spreadsheet February
Month End Spreadsheet March
Month End Spreadsheet April

Each time you open the Financials folder the file system sorts the file names front to back. Because the differences between file names are in the ending words, the process to alphabetize them takes longer than if the difference were in the front of the file names as in the following:

January Month End Spreadsheet
February Month End Spreadsheet
March Month End Spreadsheet
April Month End Spreadsheet

Planning how you name files does not create a huge speed advantage, but it can reduce the feeling of being under pressure when you have to access a file in a hurry, such as just before a meeting or during a phone call.

Another way to speed access to the files in a folder is to divide your files into more folders or subfolders, so that each one contains fewer files. For example, in a business you might currently have all of your financial files in one Financials folder, including budget files, month end files, sales files, and accounts files. You could instead divide the files into subfolders called Budget, Month End, Sales, and Accounts.

Using an External Drive

Another approach for managing large files is to store them on a fast external hard drive. The advantage of using an external hard drive is that your large files may load faster and you can take the drive with you, such as during holidays and vacations, so the files can be accessed on someone else's computer.

There are two kinds of external drives to consider: ATA and eSATA. You can easily plug these drives into the USB port on your computer (the same port you probably use to download pictures from your camera).

One type of drive uses Advanced Technology Attachment (ATA) technology (essentially the same technology your internal hard drive uses), but it attaches to a USB port on your computer. This type of external drive can hold as much information or more than your internal hard drive, such as 80 to over 200 GB.

Depending on whether you have an older (USB 1.1) or newer (USB 2.0) USB port, the data is transferred at from 480 Mbps (mega or million bits per second) to about 600 Mbps. However, the actual transfer rate will be somewhat slower because an external ATA drive is likely to require that your computer use the PIO data transfer method, which takes up CPU resources and time.

A faster option is to purchase an external Serial ATA drive (eSATA). This technology is newer than ATA and offers much faster data transfer rates. eSATA drives use the DMA data transfer method, which is fast and frees the computer's CPU for other tasks. The original SATA drives have an actual data transfer rate of about 1.2 Gbps (gigabits per second). The newer SATA II drives offer a data transfer rate of about 2.4 Gbps. Still newer SATA-IO drives will come on the market soon and offer twice the speed (4.8 Gbps) of SATA II drives.

eSATA drives are made to plug into a USB port on your computer, but you may also have to connect the drive to a wall outlet for power. If you purchase an eSATA external drive you can move your photo and other large files to any computer that has a free USB port and have fast access to those files.

Tip: Several hard drive manufacturers offer external ATA and eSATA hard drives. These include iomega (www.iomega.com), Seagate (www.seagate.com), and Western Digital (www.westerndigital.com).

Tips for Those Who Want to Work with the Registry

There are two Registry changes that are easy to implement with the result of speeding your access to the information on your computer's hard disks. These Registry changes accomplish the following:

- Give more space to the Master File Table.
- Turn off the old style MS-DOS file names.

You learn about each of these in the next sections.

Increase the Size of the Master File Table

Have you ever wondered how Windows XP keeps track of all the files on a disk? The answer is that the NT

File System used by Window XP (and other versions of Windows) creates a Master File Table (MFT). As you can image, the MFT is critical to your system. It contains all kinds of information about each file, such as security information, creation and modification dates, and size. If the MFT becomes fragmented access to files is slowed down. Also, the disk defragmentation tool in Windows XP does not defragment the MFT.

You can reduce the probability of a fragmented MFT by instructing Windows XP to increase the size of the MFT. Increasing the size helps to ensure enough space is allocated on your disk to keep the MFT in one contiguous area of the disk.

Make the following change in the Registry to increase the size of the MFT.

1. Click **Start**.
2. Click **Run**.
3. Enter **regedit** and click **OK**.
4. Open the **HKEY_LOCAL_MACHINE** folder in the left pane.
5. Open the **SYSTEM** folder in the left pane.
6. Open the **CurrentControlSet** folder in the left pane.
7. Open the **Control** folder in the left pane.
8. Open the **FileSystem** folder in the left pane.
9. Click the **Edit** menu.
10. Point to **New** and click **DWORD Value**.
11. Enter **NtfsMftZoneReservation** as the new DWORD and press **Enter**.
12. Double-click the new DWORD you created, **NtfsMftZoneReservation**.

13. Enter **2** in the **Value data:** box and click **OK**. (Note that you can enter values between 1 and 4.)
14. Close the Registry Editor.

Turn Off the Use of MS-DOS File Names

Consider turning off the compatibility with MS-DOS file names. For backward compatibility with MS-DOS and old MS-DOS applications, Windows XP supports MS-DOS file names. These are names limited to the format of up to eight characters in front of the period and 3 characters in the extension after the period—also known as 8.3 file names.

If you're not running old MS-DOS applications and do not have an old MS-DOS computer on your network, turn off the MS-DOS compatibility. Disabling 8.3 file naming can speed up access to your computer's hard disk.

Use the following steps to turn off MS-DOS file naming:

1. Click **Start**.
2. Click **Run**.
3. Enter **regedit** and click **OK**.
4. Open the **HKEY_LOCAL_MACHINE** folder in the left pane.
5. Open the **SYSTEM** folder in the left pane.
6. Open the **CurrentControlSet** folder in the left pane.
7. Open the **Control** folder in the left pane.
8. Open the **FileSystem** folder in the left pane.
9. Double-click **NtfsDisable8dot3NameCreation**.

10. Change **Value data:** to 1 (the default is 0, which enables MS-DOS file names).
11. Click **OK**.
12. Close the Registry Editor.

Chapter 4

Speed Up Network and Internet Access

Often people believe their computer is slow when the real problem is that their network access is slow. Slow network access can cause delays when you log into your computer or log onto your account. It can also slow down access to shared files or to the Internet. In this chapter, you learn how to tune your network and Internet access for faster response. If you frequently use a network or the Internet, the time saved over a week or month can be significant. Even if you don't use your network much, there is a tuning option in this chapter that can save you significant time when you access files and folders on your local computer. Try this surprising tuning option if you find that My Computer is slow to locate or access a file or folder that is on your C: drive.

Tuning Your Network Connection

Sometimes slow network access can be due to how your network connection is configured. In other cases, slow access is related to settings used by the software that drives your network interface or because you have an old version of the software. If you use a dial-up modem, a DSL adapter or hub, or a cable modem, there are also steps you can take to enable them to work at full speed. In the sections that follow, you learn how to address each of these issues.

Tune Your Address

Just as your house or apartment has an address, so does your computer when it is connected to a network or the Internet. The computer's address is called an Internet Protocol or IP address. There are two main ways an IP address is assigned for your computer. One way, which is the default, is to obtain the IP address automatically. This means that your computer contacts a special server on the network or over the Internet to obtain its IP address from a pool of addresses not being used at the time. Contacting this server and waiting to be assigned an address can take extra time—which you experience as a waiting period to log onto your account. If the server assigning the IP address has many computers asking for an address at the same time, the wait is even longer.

A faster way to get connected without the wait is to have a manually assigned IP address. With a manually assigned address, you use the same address each time you access the network. There is no waiting to contact a server to obtain an address. As the computer's user, you manually enter the IP address one time and from that time on the computer uses that address. Using a manual IP address can significantly speed up your network access when you log on.

The first step is to contact your network or Internet service provider and ask for a manual IP address you can use. The address is what is called a dotted decimal address because it consists of up to four numbers separated by periods, such as 183.201.25.101. You'll also need to obtain a subnet mask value (which consists of dotted decimal values that identify the type of network address). Your service provider may also give you a default gateway number, a preferred DNS server address, and an alternate DNS server address—all of which are also in the form of dotted decimal IP addresses. (In some cases, depending on how you access your network, your network provider may not be able to give you an IP address. If this is the case, do not make up one on your own because this can cause problems on networks, particularly if someone else is using the same address.)

Tip: When you contact your network or Internet service provider, ask if there are any drawbacks to using a manual IP address in terms of how their network is set up.

After you obtain the IP address information, use the following steps to configure your manual IP address:

Tip: It's best to close any open windows or active programs before you start the steps presented in this chapter.

1. Click **Start**.
2. Click **Control Panel**.
3. In the left pane of Control Panel, if you see *Switch to Classic View* then you are in the Category View of the Control Panel tool—stay in this view and click **Network and Internet Connections**, then click **Network Connections**. If instead you see *Switch to Category View* in the left pane of Control Panel—stay in this view and double-click the **Network Connections** icon.
4. Right-click the connection you use to access your network or the Internet, such as one of the following: **Local Area Connection**, **Wireless**

Network Connection, or **Dial-up Connection**. Click **Properties**.

5. In the box titled, This connection uses the following items:, click **Internet Protocol (TCP/IP)**.
6. Click the **Properties** button.
7. If necessary, select the **General** tab.
8. Ensure that **Use the following IP address:** is selected.
9. Enter the IP address and subnet mask as in Figure 4-1. Also, if your service provider gave you addresses for any of the following enter these addresses as well: default gateway, preferred DNS server, and alternate DNS server. (If any portion of the address is less than three characters, you can advance to enter the next number in the address by pressing the period key.)

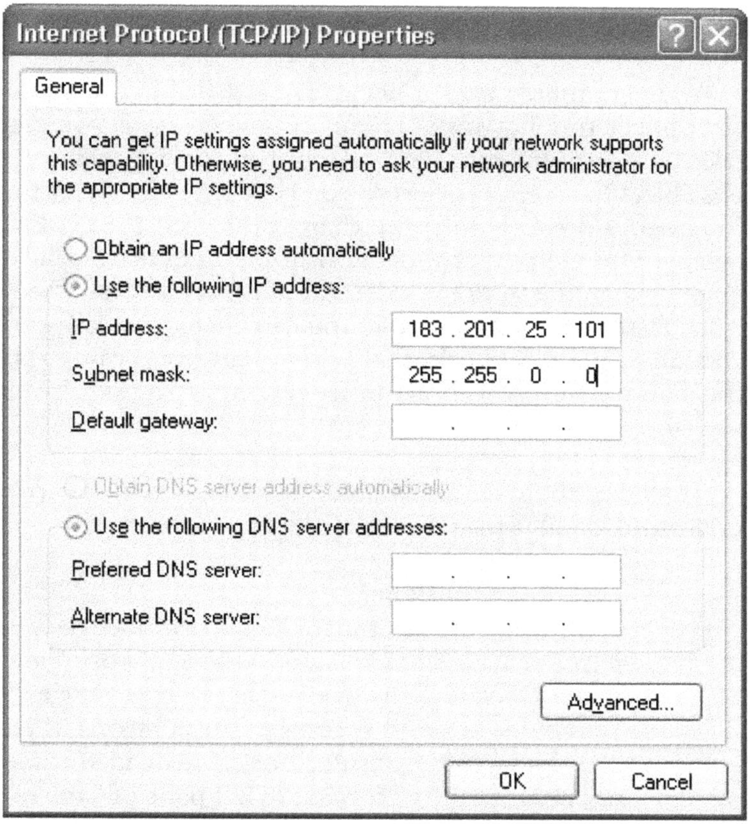

Figure 4-1: Manually configuring an IP address

10. Click **OK** in the Internet Protocol (TCP/IP) Properties dialog box.
11. Click **OK** or **Close** in the network connection Properties dialog box.
12. Close the Network Connections window.

Tune Your Network Card Connection

Your computer uses a network card or circuit board to connect to a network. There are several steps you can take to make sure your network card is working as fast as possible. One step is to ensure you have a recent driver for the card. A driver is software that works with the card to manage your network connection. Sometimes drivers have bugs or manufacturers rewrite the drivers to make them work faster and more reliably. You can check the date and version of your network card's driver and then can go to the manufacturer's Web site to see if there is a newer driver available.

To check the date and version of your network card's driver and install a new driver:

1. Click **Start**.
2. Click **Control Panel**.
3. In the left pane of Control Panel, if you see *Switch to Classic View* then you are in the Category View of the Control Panel tool—stay in this view and click **Network and Internet Connections**, then click **Network Connections**. If instead you see *Switch to Category View* in the left pane of Control Panel—stay in this view and double-click the **Network Connections** icon.
4. Right-click the appropriate network connection (if you have more than one), such as **Local Area Connection** or **Wireless Network Connection**.
5. Click **Properties**.
6. Click the **Configure** button near the top of the dialog box.
7. Click the **Driver** tab (see Figure 4-2).

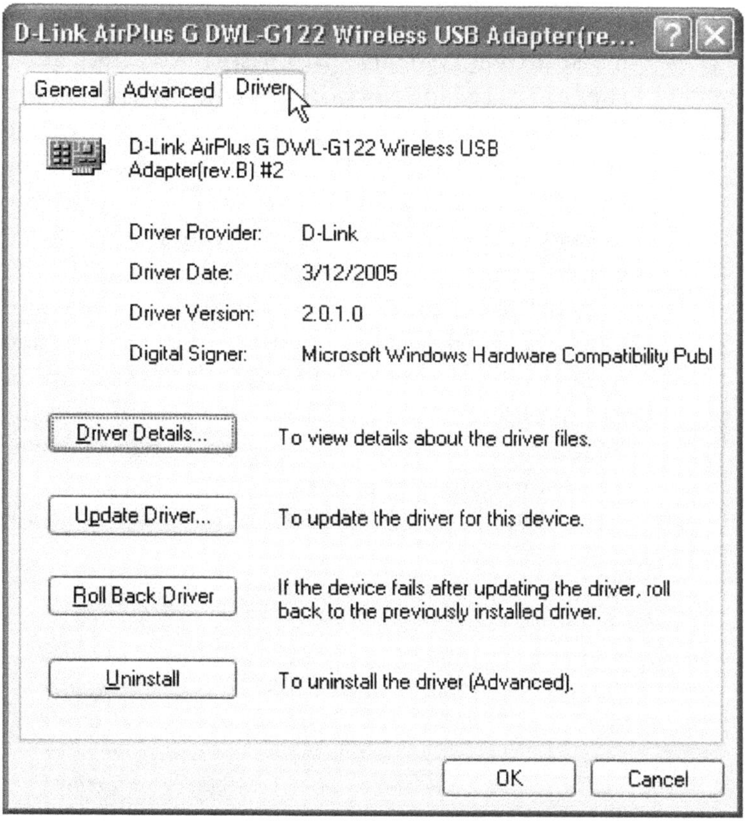

Figure 4-2: Selecting the Driver tab

8. The top portion of the tab shows the Driver Provider, Driver Date, Driver Version, and Digital Signer. Record this information.
9. At this point you can search the Windows Update Web site to see if Microsoft has an updated version of the driver. However, it is better to go directly to your network card manufacturer's or

computer manufacturer's Web site to obtain the latest driver, because Microsoft may not have the most recent version. If you choose to try the Windows Update Web site, click **Update Driver** and follow the directions provided by the Hardware Update Wizard. If you go to the network card manufacturer's Web site, look for a link to technical support, downloads, or to the network card model. Find the latest driver and compare the driver date and version you recorded with the ones for the latest driver. If your driver is an older version, follow the manufacturer's instructions for downloading an updated driver and for installing the driver.

10. Close any open windows and dialog boxes when you are done.

Tip: For Step 9, if you decide not to use the Update Driver option and if your network card or interface was already installed when you purchased your computer, first go to the computer manufacturer's Web site to find the latest driver. If it is not available there, then go to the network card manufacturer's Web site. It is not difficult to update the driver and can be well worth the effort.

Another technique for tuning your network card is to make sure the card's parameters are set optimally. For example, a wired network may be able to send and receive at the same time (full duplex communications) but a computer's network card may be set so that it can only send or receive (half duplex) at different time intervals. If your network card is set for half duplex instead of full duplex (on a full duplex network), then it is only performing at half the possible speed.

Try these steps to tune your network card's settings:

1. Follow Steps 1 through 6 in the set of steps just listed for checking the information about your network card's driver.
2. Click the **Advanced** tab (instead of the Driver tab).
3. For a wired network card set the following (the exact names of the setting options may be slightly different for different network cards):
   - If there is a flow control option under Property, set the Value box to **Enable**.
   - If there is a media type, speed, duplex, or combined speed/duplex setting, set it to automatically sense the speed and duplex modes, such as **Auto** or **AutoSelect** (see Figure 4-3). If your network card does not have an option to automatically sense the speed or duplex mode, then you'll need to find out the speed capacity of your cable. You'll also need to find out the speed of your network devices, such as a hub, switch, or router. In most cases more recently installed devices and network cable support 100 Mbps and full duplex communications.

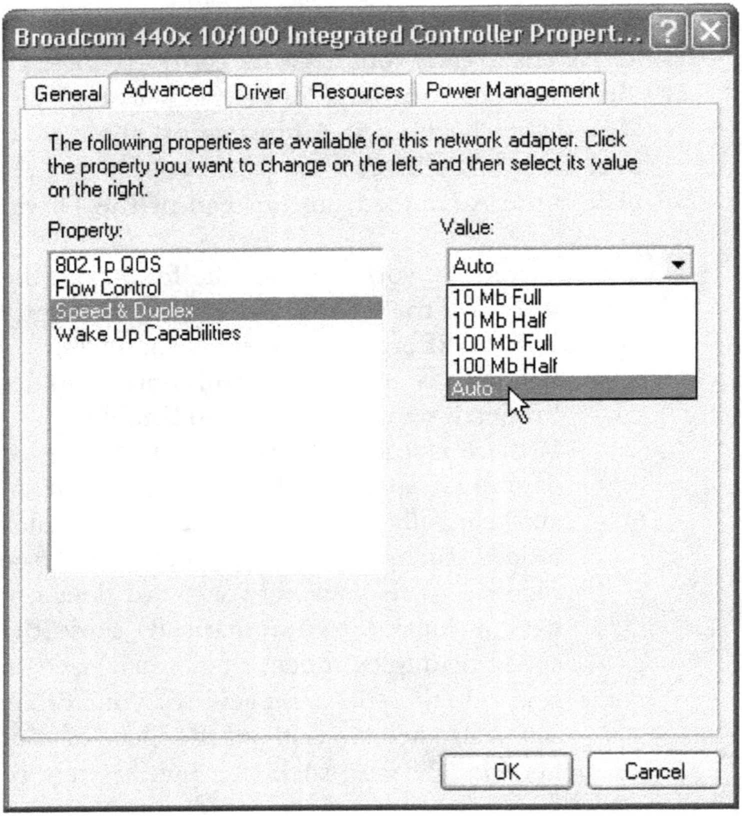

Figure 4-3: Selecting to automatically sense the connection type

For a wireless network card set these parameters (which depend on the brand and model of your card):

- If there is an Auto Reconnect mode, set the Value box to Enable, so that your card automatically reconnects if it temporarily loses the network connection.

- If there is a Network Type mode set this to match your network. For example, configure the network type to Infrastructure (see Figure 4-4) if there is a central access point—such as a wireless switch or router—or set it to 802.11 Ad Hoc if there is no access point. Alternatively, on some other wireless network cards the Network Type mode is used to identify if this is an 802.11a, 802.11b, 802.11g, or 802.11n (or combination 802.11a or g) network. Modern wireless networks are 802.11g which can transmit at up to 54 Mbps. 802.11n is a newer standard that is due to be official in mid-2007 and that can transmit over 10 times faster than 802.11g. Note you'll have more reliable and potentially faster communications if your network has a central access point. Also, combination networks that have all 802.11g or 802.11n devices (no 802.11b devices) generally operate faster (because they don't wait on the slower 802.11b wireless devices).

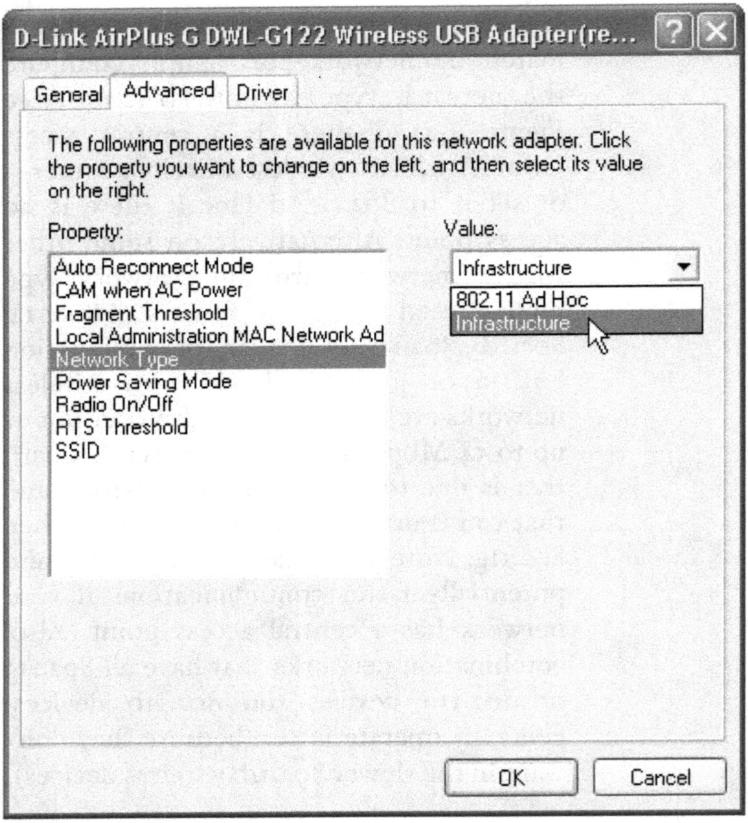

Figure 4-4: Configuring the network type

4. Click **OK**.
5. Close the Network Connections window.

Tune Your Network Protocols

Just as you use a language to communicate, your computer uses a communication language over a network.

When two computers are communicating over a network or the Internet, they use a common protocol—which is like a language. Because a network can have both older and newer computers connected to it, there may be more than one protocol in use. Some older protocols are "chatty" which means they send extra messages across the network, creating more congestion. Also, your computer may be configured to use more than one protocol, which can lead to slower communications between your computer and the network.

Consider a computer that is configured for both TCP/IP and IPX/SPX. TCP/IP is generally the protocol of choice for networks. It also is the protocol used by the Internet. IPX/SPX is a protocol used on older Novell NetWare networks, and that is no longer needed on upgraded NetWare networks. Newer NetWare networks use TCP/IP. Also, a disadvantage of IPX/SPX is that it is a chatty protocol.

You can help speed up communications between your computer and the network by eliminating all protocols except TCP/IP. (If you have a network administrator, first check to make sure that you don't need other protocols.)

To eliminate unneeded protocols:

1. Save any work and close all windows before you start.
2. Click **Start**.
3. Click **Control Panel**.
4. In the left pane of Control Panel, if you see *Switch to Classic View*, stay in this view and click **Network and Internet Connections**, then click

Network Connections. If instead you see *Switch to Category View* in the left pane of Control Panel, stay in this view and double-click the **Network Connections** icon.

5. Right-click the appropriate network connection, such as **Local Area Connection** or **Wireless Network Connection**. (If you do have more than one connection, repeat the next steps to delete unused protocols.)
6. Click **Properties**.
7. In the box entitled, *This connection uses the following items:* look for NWLink NetBIOS, NWLink IPX/SPX/NetBIOS Compatible Transport Protocol, or both. Click **NWLink IPX/SPX/NetBIOS Compatible Transport Protocol**. Click **Uninstall** (see Figure 4-5). (If both NWLink NetBIOS and NWLink IPX/SPX/NetBIOS Compatible Transport Protocol are installed click NWLink IPX/SPX/NetBIOS Compatible Transport Protocol first. Removing this protocol will also remove NWLink NetBIOS at the same time.)

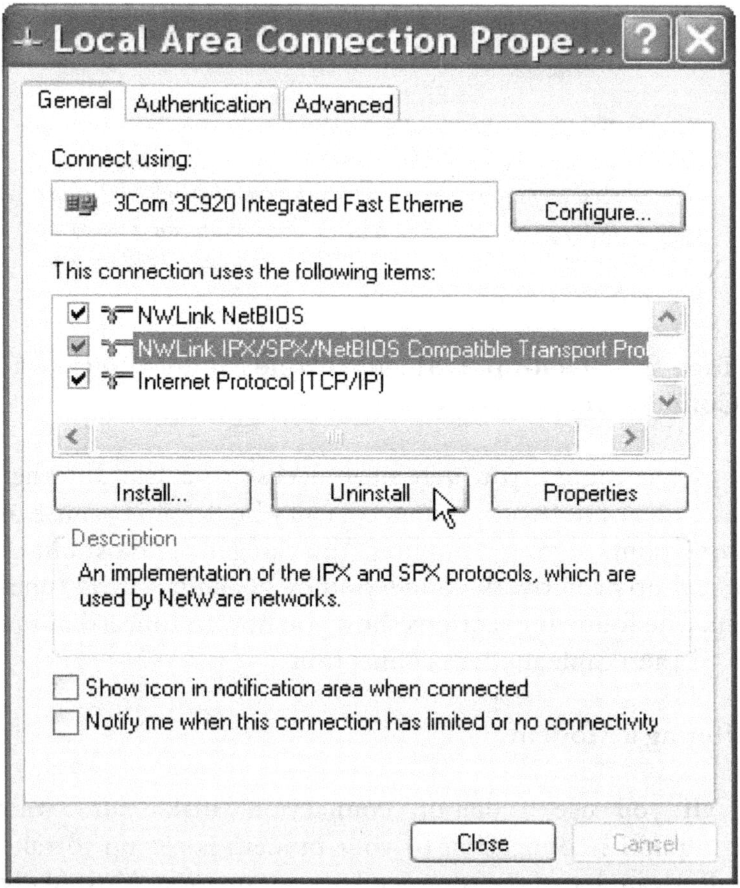

Figure 4-5: Uninstalling NWLink IPX/SPX/NetBIOS Compatible Transport Protocol

8. Click **Yes**.
9. Click **Yes** to restart the computer (it may take a couple of minutes for the computer to display the box for restarting).

10. Repeat Steps 2 through 7 to verify you have removed the unwanted protocols.

Tip: In Windows 2000 and in earlier versions of Windows, a computer may also have the NetBEUI protocol installed. You can use these steps to remove NetBEUI as well. NetBEUI is not only a chatty protocol, it has routing limitations on a network that uses routers. Eliminating NetBEUI can help speed up your network and network connection.

Tune Your Dial-up, DSL, and Cable Modem Network Connections

Even though you may have access to a fast Internet provider or network, your access may be slowed because of constraints at your computer. You can get the most out of a dial-up or network connection by giving it a little tune-up. The following sections show you how to tune a dial-up, DSL, and cable modem connection.

Tuning a Modem

If you use a dial-up connection, make sure your computer's connection to your modem is set up to take full advantage of the top speed of your modem. Most likely you have a modem that is capable of 56 Kbps (kilobytes per second) transmission over the telephone line. If you have a V.90 modem this means you really have a maximum transmission speed of 33.6 Kbps upstream coming into the modem and 56 Kbps going downstream from the computer to the network. The more recent V.92 modem has a faster maximum upstream transmission rate of 48 Kbps.

Even though your modem may be installed as a computer circuit board inside the computer it technically has two connections, one to the computer and the other to a telephone cable that goes out to a telephone connection in your residence or place of business. In some cases, the connection to your computer may be set below the maximum transmission speed of the modem, such as at 19 or 38 Kbps. (The lower speeds are available to make your computer backward compatible to older modems.) This is like placing a restrictor on your modem so that its top speed cannot go beyond 19 or 38 Kbps—much like reducing the water flow out of a hose by connecting a large diameter hose to a smaller diameter hose. Plan to check the connection speed of your computer's modem port that connects to the computer to ensure you are working at the top speed of the port.

To configure your computer's port to the modem:

1. Click **Start**.
2. Click **Control Panel**.
3. In the left pane of Control Panel, if you see *Switch to Classic View* click **Printers and Other Hardware** and then click **Phone and Modem Options**. If instead you see *Switch to Category View* in the left pane of Control Panel, stay in this view and double-click the **Phone and Modem Options** icon.
4. Click the **Modems** tab in the Phone and Modem Options dialog box.
5. Click the modem listed under the Modem column. (In some cases your computer might have more than one modem listed. If so, configure both modems using these steps.)
6. Click the **Properties** button.
7. Click the **Modem** tab.

8. Look at the Maximum Port Speed box and ensure it is set to 115200, which is the maximum setting (and well above 56 Kbps). If it is not set to this speed, click the down arrow in the Maximum Port Speed box to see the full list of speeds (see Figure 4-6). Click **115200**.

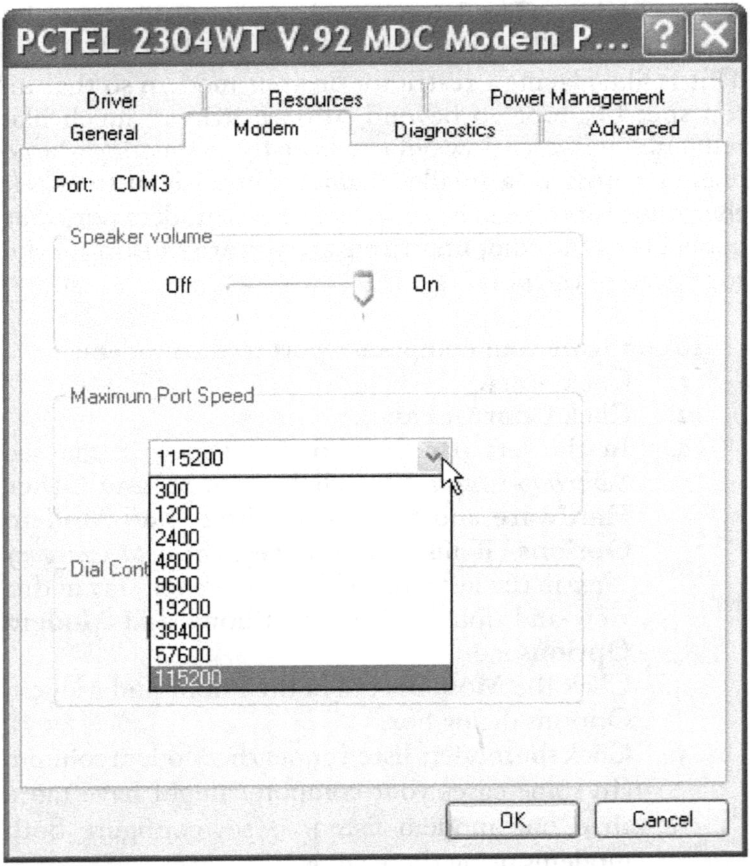

Figure 4-6: Opening the Maximum Port Speed box

9. Click the **Advanced** tab in your modem's dialog box. (Not all modems offer this feature. If there is no Advanced tab, skip to Step 13.)
10. Click the **Advanced Port Settings** button.
11. Ensure that the box for **Use FIFO buffers (requires 16550 compatible UART)** is checked. Also make sure that the slider bars for **Receive Buffer:** and **Transmit Buffer:** are both moved over as far to the right as possible—next to the high settings which are High(14) for the Receive Buffer and High(16) for the Transmit Buffer.
12. Click **OK** in the Advanced Settings dialog box.
13. Click **OK** in the modem's dialog box.
14. Click **OK** in the Phone and Modem Options dialog box.
15. Close the Printers and Other Hardware or Control Panel window, if it is still open.

Tip: You may see a message that you cannot complete the steps to configure the modem because the Telephony service is disabled. To enable and then start the service, click Start, right-click My Computer, click Manage, double-click Services and Applications in the left pane, double-click Services, scroll to Telephony and double-click it. Next, set the Startup type: to Automatic, click the Start button in the dialogue box, and click OK.

Tuning a DSL or Cable Connection

You may have a DSL or cable connection for Internet connectivity through a telephone or cable TV line. The software for your particular DSL adapter or cable modem will vary, but consider contacting your provider for help in tuning the size and/or timing of the packets (information carrying units) sent and received. Tuning these elements can speed up your Internet connection.

If you have a DSL connection that plugs into a USB port on your computer, you'll get faster service if you use a USB 2.0 port instead of a USB 1.1 port. USB 2.0 can be up to 40 times faster than USB 1.1. Check the hardware information that came with your computer to determine the type of USB ports in the computer. (Or use Device Manager to check the ports. To use Device Manager, click Start, right-click My Computer, click Manage, double-click Device Manager in the left pane, double-click Universal Serial Bus controllers in the right pane, and check out the names of the controller(s) for the USB version. A USB 2.0 port often has "USB 2.0" in the name.) If your computer has USB 1.1 ports, consider contacting a local hardware maintenance technician for an upgrade. Or, purchase a USB 2.0 adapter card (for about $50 to $100) and install it yourself in an open slot inside your computer.

If you use wireless DSL, the speed and strength of the signal is related to how far your computer is from the wireless DSL hub. The closer you are to the hub the better the connection. Check your connection rating to determine if you should consider moving the hub and computer closer to one another.

To check the connection rating for wireless DSL:

1. Click **Start**.
2. Click **Control Panel**.
3. In the left pane of Control Panel, if you see *Switch to Classic View* click **Network and Internet Connections** and then click **Network**

Connections. If you see *Switch to Category View* in the left pane of Control Panel, stay in this view and double-click the **Network Connections** icon.

4. Double-click **Wireless Network Connection**.
5. Observe the green bars to the right of Signal Strength: (see Figure 4-7). If you have five green bars, you are working at the optimum and there is no need to move the computer or DSL or cable hub. If you have only two or three green bars, consider moving the computer and hub closer to one another for a better connection (unless you are already satisfied with your connection performance or cannot move the computer and hub closer).

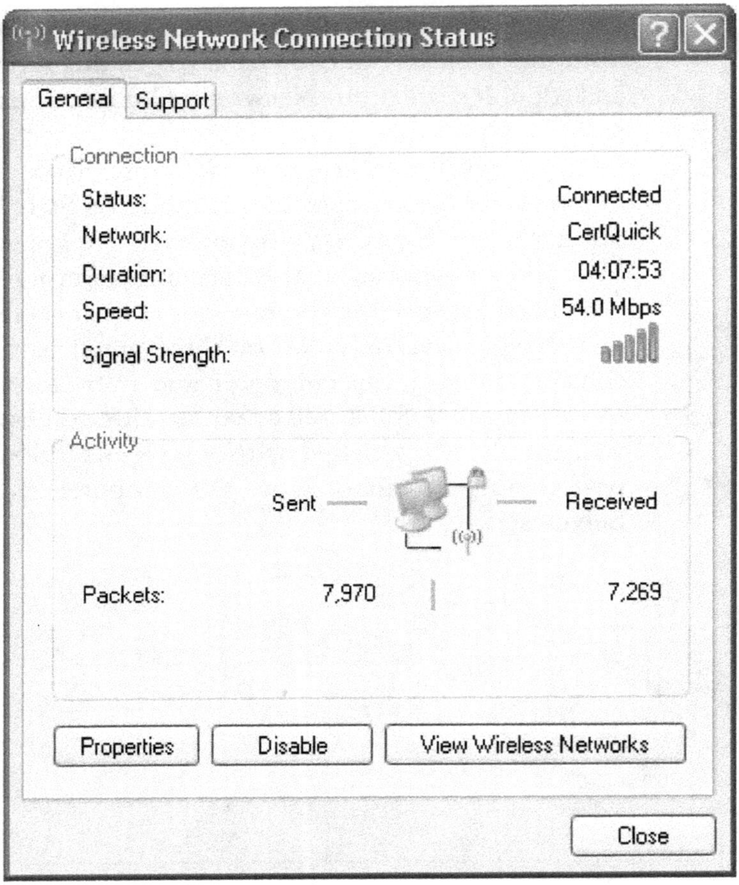

Figure 4-7: Checking the Signal Strength of a wireless connection

6. Click **Close**.
7. Close the Network Connections window, if it is still open.

Tuning Your Folder and File Access

My Computer enables you to locate and open folders and files on your computer. On your system, My Computer may wait several seconds to several minutes until it finds or opens a folder or file. For users who frequently experience delays, this can add up to lots of wasted time. The delay typically happens because your computer is spending time searching not only your computer, but the network or Internet for the folder or file you have selected. You can speed up My Computer (sometimes significantly), by turning off the option to search the network for folders and files.

Use the following steps to speed up My Computer:

1. Click **Start**.
2. Click **My Computer**.
3. Click the **Tools** menu.
4. Click **Folder** options.
5. Select the **View** tab.
6. Under Files and Folders, uncheck the box for **Automatically search for network folders and printers** (see Figure 4-8).

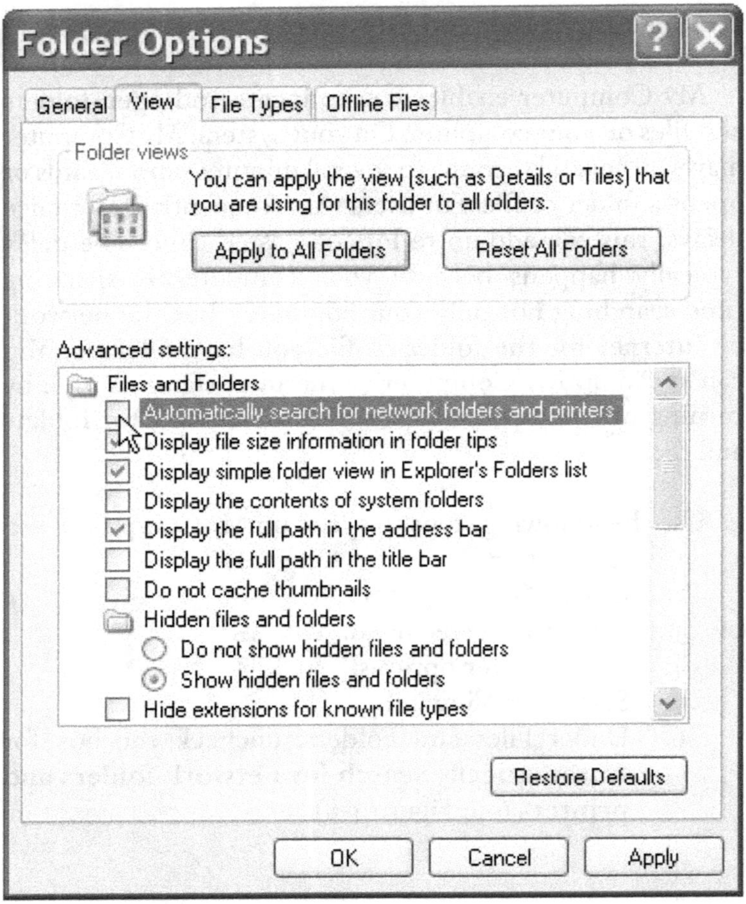

Figure 4-8: Disabling the option to search for network folders and printers

7. Click **OK**.
8. Close **My Computer**.

Tips for Those Who Want to Work with the Registry

There are two important Registry tricks for speeding your network response. One trick is to increase the Domain Name System cache size so your computer keeps track of places it has visited for a longer period of time. The second trick is to disable remote task scheduling, which is a default setting that is typically only needed by network administrators.

Expand the DNS Cache

If you frequently go to the same network places or Web sites, you can shave off some of the time it takes for your computer to find these network locations. Your computer uses something called Domain Name System (DNS) cache to store the path through the network to a specific network or Web site. DNS refers to special network servers (computers) that keep track of computer names, IP addresses, and other vital network information used to find specific computers on the network. For example, when you are in Internet Explorer or another Web browser and type in the name of a Web site, your computer contacts one or more DNS servers that change the Web site name to an IP address in a process called resolving. With the help of other DNS servers and network devices, the path to the Web site is found.

Your computer temporarily stores the resolution information to make your next connection to the same Web site faster. This information is stored in your computer's DNS cache. You can increase the size of the DNS cache so that more information is stored for a longer period of time. Expanding the DNS cache is very effective if you visit many of the same network locations repeatedly.

Here's how to expand the DNS cache in Windows XP:

1. Click **Start**.
2. Click **Run**.
3. Enter **regedit** and click **OK**.
4. Open the **HKEY_LOCAL_MACHINE** folder in the left pane.
5. Open the **SYSTEM** folder in the left pane.
6. Open the **CurrentControlSet** folder in the left pane.
7. Open the **Services** folder in the left pane.
8. Scroll down to and open the **Dnscache** folder in the left pane.
9. Open the **Parameters** folder in the left pane.
10. Click the **Edit** menu.
11. Point to **New** and click **DWORD Value**.
12. Enter **MaxCacheEntryTtlLimit** as the new DWORD and press **Enter**.
13. Double-click the new DWORD you created, **MaxCacheEntryTtlLimit**.
14. Enter **ff00** (enter zeros and not the letter "O") in the **Value data:** box and click **OK**.
15. Click the **Edit** menu.
16. Point to **New** and click **DWORD Value**.
17. Enter **MaxSOACacheEntryTtlLimit** as the new DWORD and press **Enter**.
18. Double-click the new DWORD you created, **MaxSOACacheEntryTtlLimit**.
19. Enter **12d** in the **Value data:** box and click **OK**.
20. Click the **Edit** menu.
21. Point to **New** and click **DWORD Value**.

22. Enter **CacheHashTableSize** as the new DWORD and press **Enter**.
23. Double-click the new DWORD you created, **CacheHashTableSize**.
24. Enter **180** in the **Value data:** box and click **OK**.
25. Click the **Edit** menu.
26. Point to **New** and click **DWORD Value**.
27. Enter **CacheHashTableBucketSize** as the new DWORD and press **Enter**.
28. Double-click the new DWORD you created, **CacheHashTableBucketSize**.
29. Enter **1** in the **Value data:** box and click **OK**.
30. Close the Registry Editor.

Disable Remote Task Scheduling

Sometimes your computer may slow down when you access your network. Or, it may slow down when you access a shared folder or printer on the network. You can speed things up by disabling remote scheduled tasks. Remote scheduled tasks are scheduled tasks run remotely from another computer via a network connection. Since you are most likely using a networked computer from which you do not run tasks remotely on another computer, consider disabling this capability. (Another advantage to disabling remote task scheduling is that it closes one door that a network intruder might attempt to use to access your computer.)

To disable remote scheduled tasks through the Registry:

1. Click **Start**.
2. Click **Run**.

3. Enter **regedit** and click **OK**.
4. Open the **HKEY_LOCAL_MACHINE** folder in the left pane.
5. Open the **SOFTWARE** folder in the left pane.
6. Scroll down to and open the **MICROSOFT** folder in the left pane.
7. Scroll down to and open the **Windows** folder in the left pane.
8. Open the **CurrentVersion** folder in the left pane.
9. Open the **Explorer** folder in the left pane.
10. Open the **RemoteComputer** folder in the left pane.
11. Open the **NameSpace** folder in the left pane.
12. Right-click the **{D6277990-4C6A-11CF-8D87-00AA0060F5BF}** folder in the left pane and click **Rename**.
13. Type in **Turnoff** and a space in front of the folder's name, as in **Turnoff {D6277990-4C6A-11CF-8D87-00AA0060F5BF}**. Press **Enter**.
14. Close the Registry Editor.

Chapter 5

Speed Up Your Computer Equipment

When you buy a computer with Windows XP installed it is often set up to use a general hardware configuration. This is like buying a car that has adjustable front seats, but leaving the seats set for a person of average height even though the driver is short and the front seat passenger is tall. Windows XP contains settings that can be adjusted to give your computer's hardware components a boost. In this chapter you learn how to speed up:

- Printing
- Your mouse
- CD/DVD recording
- The display monitor
- Your CPU
- Access to multimedia files

Other features that speed your computer and save time are to turn off the sound and to set up fast user switching. Turning off the sound can give you a speed edge if you don't use speakers. Fast user switching saves time and headaches when you share a computer with other people.

Faster Printing

After you send a document to a printer you may find you have to wait awhile for the printer to deliver the printout. If you are printing several documents this waiting time can be frustrating. To solve the problem most printers have a "Faster Printing," "Quick Print," or similar print setting. When you use this setting, the print quality may be slightly reduced, but chances are no one will notice.

To use the faster print option:

Tip: For the best results, close any open windows or active programs before you start the steps presented in this chapter.

1. Click **Start**.
2. Click **Control Panel**.
3. In the left pane of Control Panel, if you see *Switch to Classic View* stay in the current view and click **Printers and Other Hardware**, then click **Printers and Faxes**. If instead you see *Switch to Category View* in the left pane of Control Panel, stay in the current view and double-click the **Printers and Faxes** icon.
4. Right-click the printer you want to print faster and click **Printing Preferences**.
5. Look for a section in the dialog box that has an option for faster printing. You may have to check the options on one or more tabs. The specific tab, section, and option name will depend on the printing software provided by the manufacturer of your printer. Often you will see such an option in a tab called General or Finishing and in a section within the tab called Print Quality or Quality/Speed. For example, Figure 5-1 shows the dialog box with the Finishing tab displayed, with a section called Print Quality, and an option

called Faster Printing. Select the option to print faster.

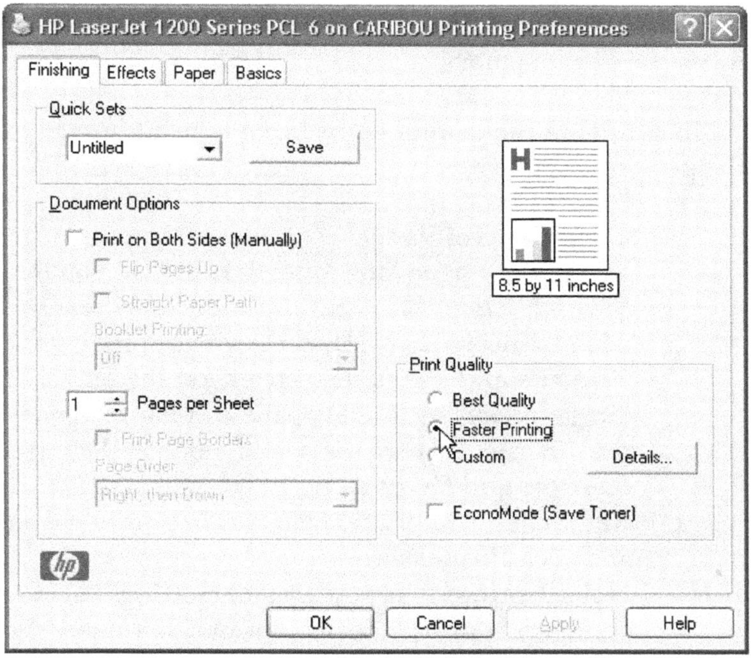

Figure 5-1: Selecting the option to print faster

6. Click **OK**.
7. Close the **Printers and Faxes window**.

If you do lots of printing, such as in an office, or you frequently print graphics or color, it can be to your advantage to add memory to your printer. More memory in a printer can equate to much faster printing, which saves time when you do a lot of printing.

Your printer may have memory slots to enable you to expand the memory to 1 GB or much more. If you add printer memory or purchase a printer that has lots of memory, make sure that you let the printer's software know it has the extra memory.

To configure the printer software to take advantage of the printer's memory:

1. Click **Start**.
2. Click **Control Panel**.
3. In the left pane of Control Panel, if you see *Switch to Classic View* stay in the current view and click **Printers and Other Hardware**, then click **Printers and Faxes**. If instead you see *Switch to Category View* in the left pane of Control Panel, stay in the current view and double-click the **Printers and Faxes** icon.
4. Right-click the printer you want to print faster and click **Properties**.
5. Not all printers have a Device Settings tab for configuring printer device options, but many do. Click the **Device Settings** tab, if your printer software offers it.

Tip: Printers that support additional memory plug-ins, multiple trays, manual paper feeding, 2-sided printing, and font cartridges are likely to have a Device Settings tab in the Properties dialog box. Some other printers have a Configure or Configuration tab on which to configure that printer's options. If you have a Configure or Configuration tab, look there for the options you can set up. Plan to configure the options in the Device Settings, Configure, or Configuration tab to take full advantage of your printer's capabilities. Note that the specific actions in Steps 6—8 may vary for setting options on a Configure or Configuration tab—but start by looking for a Printer Memory box you can configure.

6. Look for a folder labeled Installable Options and then look for Printer Memory listed under this folder.
7. Click **Printer Memory**.
8. Click the down arrow for the Printer Memory list box and select the amount of memory contained in your printer (see Figure 5-2).

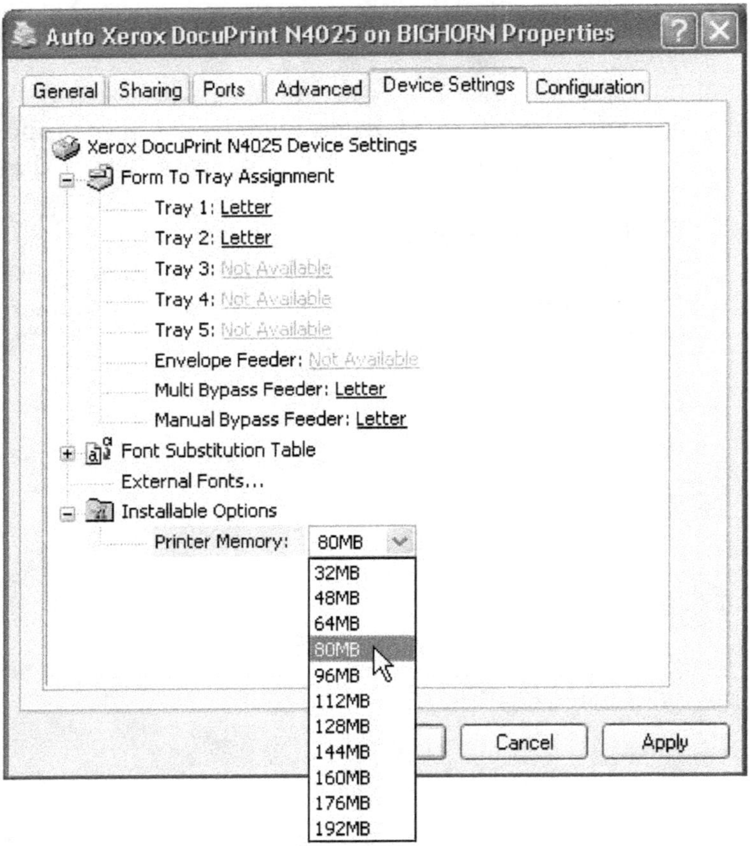

Figure 5-2: Configuring the amount of printer memory

9. Click **OK**.
10. Close the Printers and Faxes window.

Speeding Up Your Mouse

Does your mouse or pointing device seem slow when you drag its pointer from one area of the screen to another? If this problem is hindering your computer productivity, you can easily remedy it by adjusting the pointer speed. Setting up the mouse pointer to move faster is one of the most easily accomplished productivity improvements.

To adjust the mouse pointer:

1. Click **Start**.
2. Click **Control Panel**.
3. In the left pane of Control Panel, if you see *Switch to Classic View* stay in the current view and click **Printers and Other Hardware**, then click **Mouse**. If instead you see *Switch to Category View* in the left pane of Control Panel, stay in the current view and double-click the **Mouse** icon.
4. Click the **Pointer Options** tab.
5. Near the top of the dialog box you'll see an option to **Select a pointer speed:**. Move the slider bar toward the Fast setting on the right (see Figure 5-3) to increase the pointer speed.

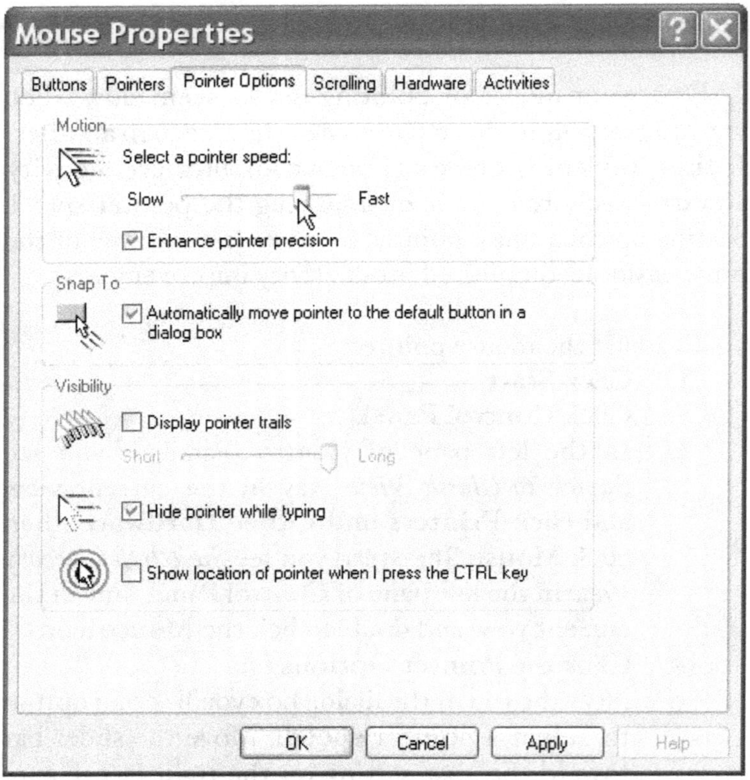

Figure 5-3: Setting the pointer speed

6. Click **Apply** and test the pointer speed to ensure it suits you. If you want the pointer to go faster or slower, move the slider bar again to match your needs.
7. Ensure that the box is checked for **Enhance pointer precision**.
8. Click **OK**.
9. Close the Printers and Other Hardware or Control Panel window.

Faster CD/DVD Recording

If you are like most people, you probably use your CD/DVD drive for recording music, copying photos, saving files, or creating backups. Waiting to burn a disc can be time consuming and frustrating, because you have other things to do. One way to make the process go faster is to ensure that the recording speed for the CD/DVD drive is set high enough.

Here's how to set the recording speed for a CD/DVD drive:

1. Click **Start**.
2. Click **My Computer**.
3. Right-click your CD/DVD drive and click **Properties**.
4. Click the **Recording** tab.
5. Find the list box for setting the recording speed. The list box will be near the bottom of the dialog box.
6. Click the down arrow to view the selections (see Figure 5-4).

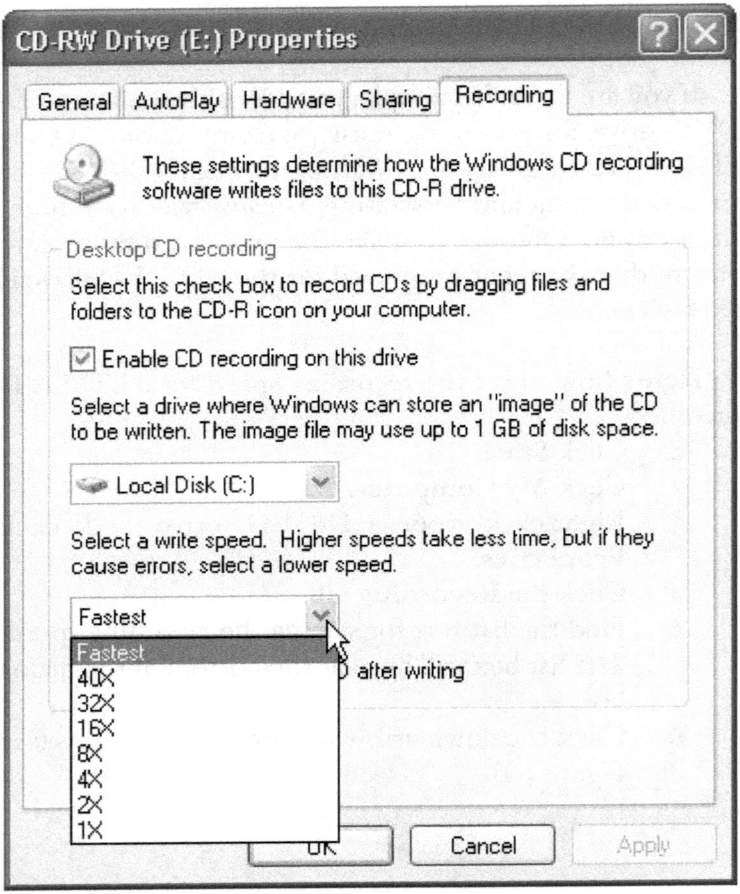

Figure 5-4: Setting the recording speed

7. Ensure that the highest speed is selected or select **Fastest**.
8. Click **OK**.
9. Close My Computer.

Faster Monitor Response

Placing images and colors on your monitor can slow your computer's response. When you first got your computer you perhaps saw a note on its monitor about setting the resolution to take full advantage of the monitor's capabilities—and so you probably set up your computer this way. Or, maybe your computer already came configured. The problem with using high resolution and color settings is that they slow down your computer. They also often make the screen harder to see. This is like buying a fast car. You typically don't need all that speed under the hood.

For example, your monitor may support a screen resolution of 1280 by 1024 pixels or 1600 by 1200 pixels and up to 32-bit color quality. If you want faster monitor response and to make it easier to see your screen's contents, consider using 1024 by 768 pixels (or another lower setting that suits your eyes) for the resolution and 16-bit color—or just use 1024 by 768 pixels and leave the color quality at 32-bit if you need more color hues.

Try these steps to change the settings for your monitor:

1. Save and close any work you have started.
2. Click **Start**.
3. Click **Control Panel**.
4. In the left pane of Control Panel, if you see *Switch to Classic View* stay in the current view and click **Appearance and Themes**, then click **Display**. If instead you see *Switch to Category View* in the left pane of Control Panel, stay in the current view and double-click the **Display** icon.

5. Click the **Settings** tab.
6. Move the slider bar under Screen resolution to set it at **1024 by 768** pixels.

Tip: You can use another setting that is lower than the maximum and higher than 1024 by 768, but the result may not be suitable for your specific monitor. You may want to experiment with the exact setting when you get to Step 9, to see what is right for you.

7. If you don't need all kinds of color hues, then set the Color quality list box to **Medium (16 bit)** (if you don't have 16-bit then choose 24-bit if that is the lowest selection). Figure 5-5 illustrates how to change the display settings.

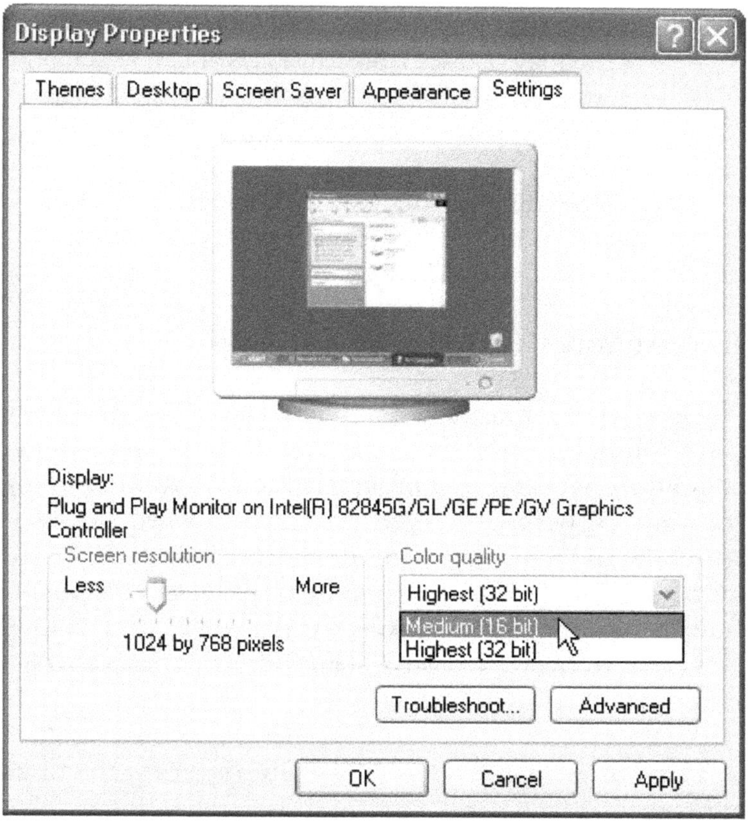

Figure 5-5: Configuring the display settings

8. Click **Apply**.
9. Wait a moment for the display to make the adjustment. Your display may go blank for a short time. You'll see a box that says: "Your desktop has been reconfigured. Do you want to keep these settings?" If you like the new settings click **Yes**. If you don't like the new settings click **No** or wait

10 seconds to revert back to the original settings. (You may also see a box that says you have selected a non-optimal screen resolution. Click **OK**. It is fine to leave this resolution as long as it suits you.)

10. Depending on the Control Panel view you have used, close the Appearance and Themes window or the Control Panel window.

Increase Your CPU's Handling of Tasks

Have you ever noticed that when you're in a real hurry your computer isn't? Let's say you're in a spreadsheet computing data and your processor seems slow in handling the work. Or, perhaps you're in your favorite word processor searching and replacing words or checking the spelling and it's taking forever. Or, your computer's processor just seems slow in responding to whatever tasks you're performing. You can give the CPU a bit of a jump start to process tasks faster.

Here's how to give your CPU a jump start for the tasks at hand:

1. Click **Start**.
2. Click **Run**.
3. In the Open: box type **Rundll32.exe advapi32.dll,ProcessIdleTasks** (see Figure 5-6).
4. Click **OK**.

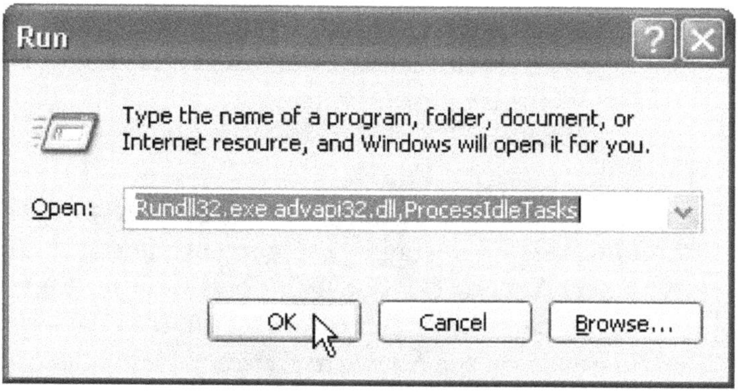

Figure 5-6: Giving your CPU a jump start

Using Fast User Switching

Sharing a computer with others can be inconvenient. At home you may have a computer that you share with another family member for games, homework, finances, and other activities. In the workplace, you may share a centrally located computer with several other workers. It can be a pain stopping your applications to log off so that another person can log on. For instance, you might be reading your e-mail when someone else comes in and needs to print a document.

The answer to this situation is to configure your computer for fast user switching. Fast user switching lets two or more people switch from one user account to another without closing any applications. If you have your e-mail open and your family member comes in to print a document, there is no need to close your e-mail. Your family member can instantly switch to his or her account, print the document and then you can switch to your account right back into your e-mail.

You can set up fast user switching using these steps:

1. Log on as administrator or access an account that has administrator privileges.
2. Click **Start**.
3. Click **Control Panel**.
4. In the left pane of Control Panel, if you see *Switch to Classic View* stay in the current view and click **User Accounts**. For Windows Home Edition users, click **User Accounts** again, if necessary. If instead you see *Switch to Category View* in the left pane of Control Panel, stay in the current view and double-click the **User Accounts** icon.
5. Click **Change the way users log on or off**.
6. Ensure that **Use the Welcome screen** is selected.
7. Check the box for **Use Fast User Switching** (see Figure 5-7).

Tip: Fast user switching is not compatible with the use of offline files. Offline files is an option in Windows XP Professional for mobile users so that shared files are available during those times when a mobile computer is not connected to the network. Some businesses that share files between computers use the offline files option. When offline files are enabled and you try to configure fast user switching, you'll see the message: "Fast User Switching cannot be used because Offline Files is enabled. To make changes to Offline Files settings, click OK." Click Cancel, if you want to continue using offline files, but not fast user switching. If you want to disable offline files and employ fast user switching, click OK, remove the check from the Enable Offline Files box, and click OK.

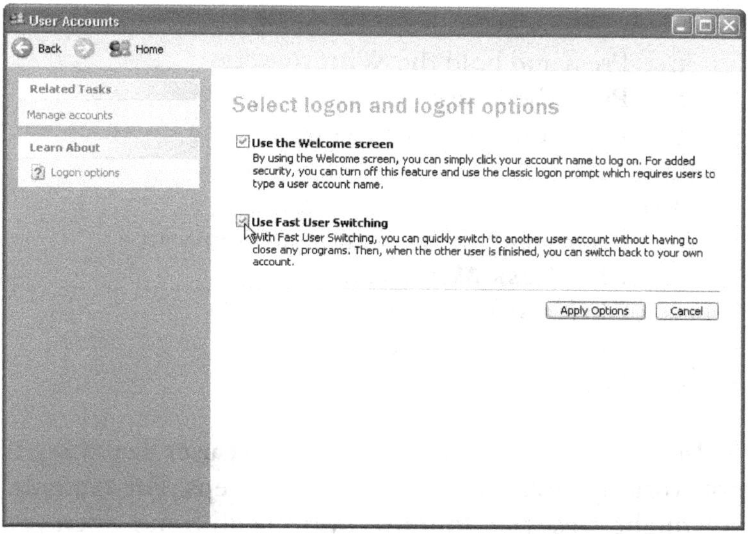

Figure 5-7: Implementing fast user switching

8. Click **Apply Options**.
9. Close the User Accounts window(s) or Control Panel.

After you have configured the fast user switching capability there are three ways to use it when someone is already logged on: from the Start menu, from the keyboard, and from Task Manager.

To switch to a different user account from the Start menu:

1. Click **Start**.
2. Click **Log Off**.
3. Click **Switch User**.
4. Log onto the other account.

To switch users from the keyboard:

1. Press and hold the **Windows key**.
2. Press the **L** key.
3. Log onto the other account.

To switch using Task Manager:

1. Right-click the taskbar in an empty area.
2. Click **Task Manager**.
3. Click the **Shut Down** menu.
4. Click **Switch User**.
5. Log onto the other account.

In some cases you may find that fast user switching is not working after you complete these steps. For example, you might press the Windows button and L and when you click Switch User, nothing happens. If so, you need to start some services required for fast user switching. Don't worry, it's easy to start these services and set them up so that they always start automatically when you boot your computer. (The time these services add to your computer's startup is minimal and is worth it when you share your computer.)

To start the services required for fast user switching:

1. Click **Start**.
2. Right-click **My Computer** and click **Manage**.
3. Double-click **Services and Applications** in the left pane.
4. Double-click **Services** in the left pane (under Services and Applications).
5. In the right pane, scroll to find **Terminal Services** and then double-click this service option.
6. Click the down arrow for the **Startup type:** list box and select **Automatic** (if Automatic is not

already selected) as in Figure 5-8. Click the **Apply** button. Click the **Start** button in the Terminal Services Properties (Local Computer) dialog box (if it is not activated, you'll need to reboot the computer after you complete these steps). Click **OK**.

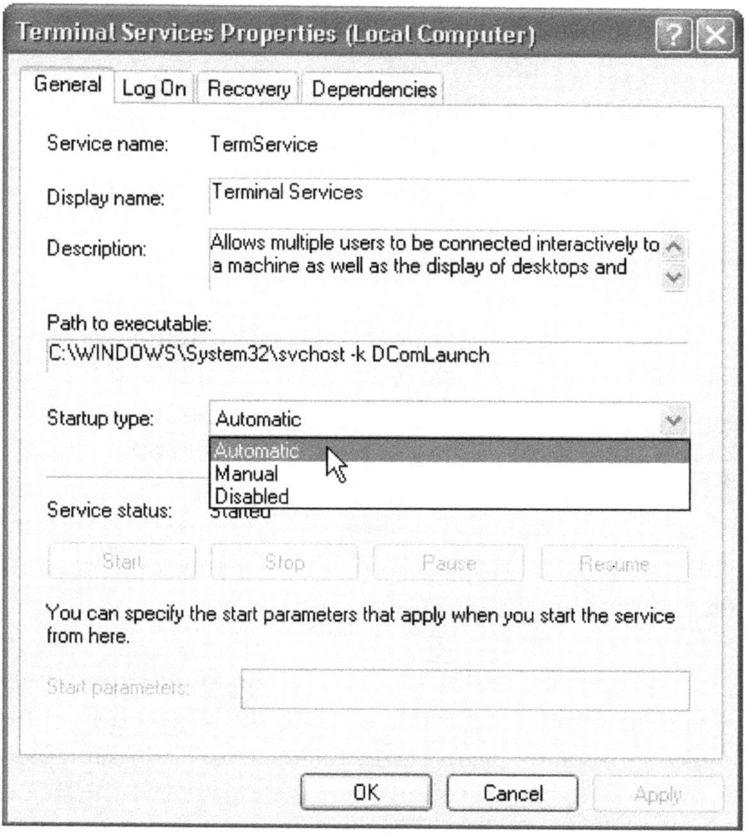

Figure 5-8: Setting Terminal Services to start automatically

7. In the right pane, scroll to find **Fast User Switching Compatibility** and double-click this service option.
8. Click the down arrow for the **Startup type:** list box and select **Automatic** (if Automatic is not already selected). Click the **Apply** button. Click the **Start** button in the **Fast User Switching Compatibility Properties (Local Computer)** dialog box (if it is not activated, you'll need to reboot the computer after you complete these steps). Click **OK**.
9. Close the Computer Management window.

Disabling Sound

When you log into your account, the computer plays a brief bit of music. Music is also played when you log out. And, as you use applications you hear beeps and other sounds, such as the sound of a cash register when you use Quicken or beeps when you perform searches in Microsoft Word. These sounds can slow the computer's response. This can be most pronounced when you are in a hurry to log on or log off the computer.

If you don't use or don't care about the sound capabilities of your computer, consider turning the sound off at the source. This can particularly make sense in your place of business, because sounds and playing music might be considered distracting to others. It also makes sense for computers used in a small office or home business.

To disable the sounds from your sound card:

1. Click **Start**.
2. Click **Control Panel**.
3. In the left pane of Control Panel, if you see *Switch to Classic View* stay in the current view and click **Sounds, Speech, and Audio Devices**, then click **Sounds and Audio Devices** (or click **Change the sound scheme**). If instead you see *Switch to Category View* in the left pane of Control Panel, stay in the current view and double-click the **Sounds and Audio Devices** icon.
4. Make sure the **Sounds** tab is displayed.
5. Click the **list arrow** in the **Sound scheme:** box to list its contents.
6. Click **No Sounds** (see Figure 5-9).

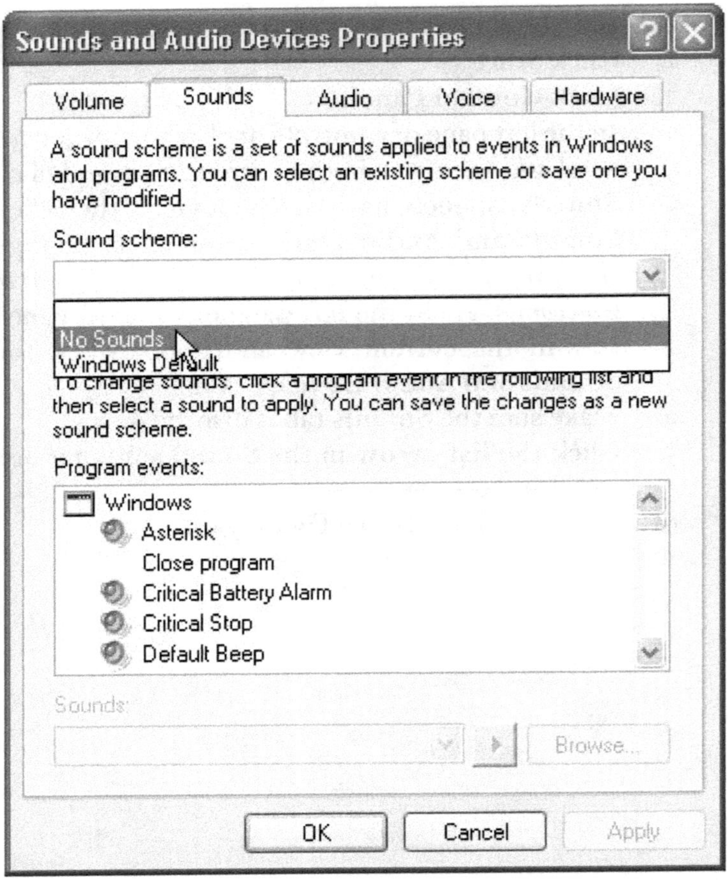

Figure 5-9: Selecting No Sounds

7. If asked to save the previous scheme, click **Yes** and provide a name for the sound scheme, such as **Original Scheme** and click **OK**.
8. Click **OK**.
9. Close the Sounds, Speech, and Audio Devices window or the Control Panel window.

Tips for Those Who Want to Work with the Registry

If you store audio/visual files on your computer, such as movie clips or instructional clips for software, try the following Registry trick to make your files easier to open.

Speeding Access to AVI Multimedia Files

Many people like to store and play audio/visual files on their computers. These files may contain a family movie clip, a news clip, or another kind of combined video and audio clip. For example, if you watch a news clip on the Internet from a major news site, you are accessing an audio/visual file.

Some audio/visual files are packaged in a format developed by Microsoft called Audio Video Interleave or AVI. You can tell if you have AVI files in a folder by looking for the .avi extension in the name of the file. (If My Computer is not configured to show file extensions you can view them by clicking Start, clicking My Computer, clicking the Tools menu, clicking Folder Options, clicking the View tab, unchecking the box for *Hide extensions for known file types*, and clicking OK).

It can take some time to open a folder in My Computer that contains lots of AVI files, because when you open the folder Windows XP obtains information about the contents of each AVI file. Also, if there is a problem with the formatting of an AVI file within a folder, Windows XP can get bogged down or stuck when trying to open the folder containing the file. You can speed up access to a folder containing AVI files by telling Windows XP to skip

www.ingramcontent.com/pod-product-compliance
Lightning Source LLC
Chambersburg PA
CBHW071201050326
40689CB00011B/2205
* 9 7 8 1 4 1 9 6 2 8 4 2 9 *